Developing Co-occurring Assessments and Treatment Plans

Jason White, EdD, MS, CCS

DEVELOPING CO-OCCURRING ASSESSMENTS AND TREATMENT PLANS

Prep Group, LLC
Rockland, ME

Send correspondence to:
jwhite@prepgroup.info

ISBN: 978-1-7358944-3-0

Update 2

Table of Contents

Preface

The inspiration for this book comes from my many years of experience in the mental health and substance abuse field, working as a regulator, provider, and administrator. Some of my first jobs in the field were as a public guardian of public wards and class member public wards, and later as a licensing agent supervisor of behavioral health programs across Maine. Eventually, I left state work, to start a non-profit organization, that became a multi-million-dollar organization; still in business today, years after I resigned. I operated this organization for about 10 years before leaving to teach in the university system.

During my tenure as an executive director, and because of an extreme right-wing government, we were consistently audited. Over the years, I have been told by state officials that my records were the best they have seen. In many instances, during audits, my organization received no citations, which is rare for organizations. There have been times when organizations requested copies of my client records, to use for their organization, which I was always open to. I am a firm believer that there is plenty of work to do, for everyone who wants to be a provider, to be successful.

In this book, I attempt to demonstrate how to write a regulatory-compliant assessment, treatment plan, and other required documents in the client and patient file, and how to put the client and patient file together. Citation trends and pitfalls are also discussed throughout the book. I hope that providers and students use the teachings in this book, and use, or develop forms, as outlined in this book. I do permit all parts of this book to be used for treatment or educational purposes.

Dr. Jason White

1. Introduction

Mental health and substance use disorders (SUDs) are prevalent and complex conditions that significantly impact individuals, families, and communities. These disorders are often characterized by a range of symptoms, including emotional distress, impaired functioning, and the use of substances that negatively affect health and well-being. Complete, accurate, and comprehensive assessment is crucial for identifying and understanding these disorders, informing treatment planning, and evaluating treatment outcomes.

Main Points

Mental health and SUD assessment play a pivotal role in various aspects of healthcare services. It provides a framework for:

Early Identification and Diagnosis: Timely identification of mental health and SUDs enables early intervention, which can significantly improve treatment outcomes and reduce the long-term burden of these disorders.

Comprehensive Understanding: Assessment helps to gain a comprehensive understanding of the individual's mental health and SUD presentation, including the severity of symptoms, underlying causes, and contributing factors.

Treatment Planning: Assessment informs treatment planning by identifying specific treatment targets and tailoring interventions to the individual's needs and strengths.

Treatment Monitoring: Assessment facilitates ongoing monitoring of treatment progress, allowing for adjustments to treatment plans as needed.

Evaluation of Treatment Outcomes: Assessment enables the evaluation of treatment effectiveness, providing valuable data for improving treatment approaches and informing clinical decision-making.

Mental health and SUD assessment is a multifaceted process that involves a range of tools and approaches. These tools are designed to gather information about the individual's mental health and substance use history, current symptoms, and overall functioning. Common assessment components include:

Records Reviews: A review of available records should occur before the clinical interview. The reason for this is so that you are aware of the traumas and triggers reported, as well as pertinent psychiatric, substance use disorder information, and other pertinent information.

Clinical Interview: A structured clinical interview conducted by a mental health professional allows for in-depth exploration of the individual's experiences, thoughts, and feelings.

Self-Report Measures: Standardized self-report questionnaires assess the severity of symptoms, patterns of substance use, and psychosocial functioning.

Diagnostic Criteria: Diagnostic criteria from established classification systems, such as the Diagnostic and Statistical Manual of Mental Disorders (DSM-5), are used to determine the presence of specific mental health or SUD diagnoses.

Collateral Information: Information from family members, caregivers, or other relevant individuals can provide valuable insights into the individual's behavior and functioning.

Assessment findings serve as a critical guide for developing and implementing effective treatment plans. By understanding the individual's unique needs and strengths, healthcare providers can tailor treatment interventions to address specific targets and maximize treatment outcomes. Assessment also facilitates ongoing monitoring and evaluation, enabling providers to adjust treatment plans as needed.

A comprehensive treatment approach for mental health and SUDs often involves a combination of psychotherapy and pharmacotherapy. Psychotherapy, such as cognitive-behavioral therapy (CBT), can help individuals identify and change negative thoughts and behaviors that contribute to their symptoms. Pharmacotherapy, such as medications for depression or anxiety, can help alleviate symptoms and improve functioning.

For individuals with SUDs, treatment may also include detoxification, which involves safely managing the withdrawal process from substances, and ongoing relapse prevention strategies. Support groups and peer support programs can provide additional support and encouragement.

The combination of psychotherapy/counseling and pharmacology is delicate. It is important to get this right as too much of one will destabilize the client. Medication is likely to play a prominent role at the beginning of treatment so that the client can benefit from psychotherapy/counseling; later, psychotherapy/counseling will play a greater role, while medication becomes less prominent.

Conclusion

Mental health and SUD assessment is an essential component of effective treatment for complex and often co-occurring disorders. By identifying and understanding the individual's unique presentation, healthcare providers can tailor treatment interventions to address specific targets and maximize treatment outcomes. Ongoing assessment and monitoring are crucial for evaluating treatment effectiveness and making adjustments as needed. With comprehensive assessment and individualized treatment, individuals with mental health and SUDs can achieve significant improvement in their quality of life and overall well-being.

2. Maine History of Assessment

Introduction

The history of psychiatric treatment in Maine has evolved over time, reflecting the changing understanding of mental illness (and substance use treatment), and the development of new treatment approaches. Many of the trends in Maine followed those of the country. During the 1960s, deinstitutionalization philosophies swept across the country. By the 1970s, Maine had successfully deinstitutionalized its psychiatric population. This led to increased rates of homelessness, exposure to violence, increased rates of serious infections (HIV and hepatitis), arrests and legal problems, and an increase in the use of drugs and alcohol.

The State continued to keep its psychiatric hospitals open, however, there were problems. State-employed providers were accused of being inadequately trained, continuing unnecessary hospitalization, using excessive restraint and seclusions, not providing individual treatment, not providing access to necessary services (such as medical treatment), and failing to protect residents from harm (physical and sexual abuse from client to client and staff to client). These claims were based on the experiences of numerous Augusta Mental Health Institute (AMHI) residents who had suffered from the alleged substandard care and treatment, which became the foundation of a class action lawsuit filed against the state. The lawsuit sought to hold the State of Maine accountable for its failure to provide adequate care for individuals with mental illness and to reform the mental health system.

Dual diagnosis and co-occurring treatment also emerged in the late 1980s and were embraced by Maine in the 1990s. The terminology was derived to describe those with both serious mental illness and substance use disorders. The risks associated with co-occurring disorders are significant and are also linked with increased rates of hospitalization (both psychiatric and medical), homelessness, poverty, arrests, violence and trauma, HIV and hepatitis infection, and poor psychosocial functioning. Maine requires all mental health and substance use treatment to be co-occurring.

Main Points

Prominent moments in Maine's history of providing mental health and SUD treatment over the years have shaped the field into what it is today. Maine has impressive and robust mental health and SUD treatment programming that must be safeguarded by providers, for the future. The following are just some of the hard-fought battles, every provider should be aware of:

Early Developments (1840-1920)

In 1840, the Maine Insane Hospital (later renamed the Augusta Mental Health Institute) opened its doors, becoming the state's first psychiatric institution. The hospital was designed to provide a humane and therapeutic environment for individuals with mental illnesses, in contrast to the harsh conditions of many asylums at the time. Treatment methods during this period were limited and often included isolation, restraint, and hydrotherapy.

Mid-Century Innovations (1920-1960)

The early 20th century saw the introduction of new treatment methods, including psychopharmacology and electroconvulsive therapy (ECT). These developments offered more effective interventions for mental health disorders and helped to improve the lives of many clients. However, these treatments were not without their controversies, and some individuals experienced adverse side effects.

Deinstitutionalization and Community Services (1960s-Present)

In the 1960s, a movement towards deinstitutionalization gained momentum, advocating for the care of people with mental illness in community settings rather than large institutions. This movement was driven by concerns about the dehumanizing effects of asylums and the potential for clients to receive more personalized care in the community.

Maine was one of the first states to implement deinstitutionalization, and by the 1980s, the Augusta Mental Health Institute had significantly reduced its hospitalization client population. However, deinstitutionalization also presented challenges, as many individuals struggled to adjust to life outside of the hospital and access adequate community-based services.

Rights of Recipients (1984 to Present)

The rights of recipients are a prominent document within the mental health and substance use disorder field. Treatment rights are often established at hospitals, organizations, and centers; however, in Maine, the 110th Maine Legislature enacted a law that required the Maine Department of Health and Human Services (DHHS) to promulgate rights for recipients of mental health care. The Legislature intended to provide a process whereby DHHS would be the lead administrative agency for institutional and community mental health services, and they would develop comprehensive rules, considering clinical, social, and administrative factors, while promoting and safeguarding the rights of people receiving mental health services.

The rules are titled 14-193 CMR Chapter 1: Rights or Recipients of Mental Health Services and can be accessed on the Maine Secretary of State website (we will go over how to access rules later in the book). The Rights apply to all agencies licensed by DHHS and all public or private inpatient psychiatric institutes and units, including those operated by DHHS. The Rights were developed by a task force made up of consumers, providers, regulators, professionals, family members, and advocates, throughout the state. The Rights were initially promulgated on October 1, 1984, were amended on October 1, 1986, October 1, 1989, and January 1, 1995. Some of the rights are:

- Recipients have the same human, civil, and legal rights as all citizens.

- Recipients have the right to a humane environment, to be treated with courtesy and dignity, and to have their privacy protected.

- Recipients shall not be denied any rights or privileges due to their status as recipients of mental health services.

- Recipients have the right to refuse or accept services, with limited exceptions.

- Recipients with long-term mental illnesses have additional rights, including a comprehensive array of services and the maintenance of natural support systems.

- Recipients have the right to be treated in the least restrictive appropriate setting to meet their needs.

- Recipients have the right to be informed of their rights, including the right to name a designated representative and the availability of advocacy programs.

- Recipients have the right to assistance in the protection of their rights.

- Recipients have the right to file grievances and complaints without reprisal.

- Recipients have the right to confidentiality and access to their records.

- Recipients have the right to be paid a fair wage for work done.

- Recipients have the right to refuse to participate in experimentation and research without loss of services.

- Recipients have the right to informed consent for all treatment and or services.

Most organizations provide a summary of the rights to their clients and have the client sign a copy for the record and auditing. The Rights are also required to be reviewed with providers, by their employer, before working with clients. This is normally documented in the personnel file, with the provider signing a summary of the rights, at the bottom of the form, with the date, or on a separate line created for the provider. Examples of these rights documents can be found in the back of the book in Appendix A.

Licensing of Mental Health Facilities (1980, 1987, 1989, 1991, 1993, 1996 to Present)

The Licensing of Mental Health Facilities rules are located on the Maine Secretary of State's website, and is filed under 14-193 CMR Chapter 6 Licensing of Mental Health Facilities (we will go over locating them more later). Under Title 34-B, Maine's mental health law, all incorporated organizations providing mental health services, must be licensed through DHHS.

The rules can be used to develop your own mental health and SUD agency. To write a policy, simply type out each rule, then respond to it by stating what your agency is doing to comply with the rule. This is the best way to write policies; by simply copying the regulation and making it your own (you may not subtract from the rule, however, you may add to it).

A few other important things about the regulation are that it requires DHHS to provide 'Technical Assistance' if it is requested. If DHHS does not respond, they may have difficulty enforcing that part of the regulation. Always note the date and time technical assistance was requested, and in what form (a copy of an email or letter is best). Additionally, some or all rules can be waived. The regulation states specifically, that while all agencies are required to comply with all regulatory requirements, protocols have been established to allow agencies to apply for waivers of one or more of these requirements [rules].

In the beginning of the regulation, the justification is eloquently established; it states:

> "A regulation is justifiable if it offers more advantage than the economic waste that it entails. Voluntary standards, if they exist, may avoid government regulation. One of the first advantages of standardization is that it enables public authorities to limit regulations to cases where compulsion is essential. Standardization thus economizes on the making of regulations. Government departments are thereby relieved of a mass of detailed work based on thousands of minor decisions. The Division of Licensing of Maine's Department of Mental Health and Mental Retardation (DMHMR)[now DHHS] is responsible for conducting licensing reviews of mental health services in the State of Maine. The mission of the Division of Licensing is as follows: To assure the public trust in the mental health

and mental retardation service delivery systems, through the application of effective, efficient, equitable, and predictable monitoring, evaluation and improvement processes. Licensing seeks to assure that agencies have an adequate capacity to provide services. It evaluates agency and client management practices, including compliance with client rights protocols."

AMHI Consent Decree (1988 to Present)

The AMHI Consent Decree lawsuit was filed in Maine on August 2, 1989. It was a class-action lawsuit brought by Disability Rights Maine (DRM) on behalf of current and former residents of the Augusta Mental Health Institute (AMHI). The lawsuit alleged that AMHI had violated the rights of its residents by providing them with substandard care and treatment. The specific claims included:

1. **Unnecessary institutionalization:** The lawsuit argued that AMHI was unnecessarily institutionalizing individuals with mental illness, many of whom could have been treated in community-based settings.

2. **Inadequate staffing:** The lawsuit alleged that AMHI was understaffed, which resulted in inadequate care and supervision for residents.

3. **Use of excessive restraint and seclusion:** The lawsuit claimed that AMHI was using excessive restraint and seclusion, which could be harmful to residents' physical and mental health.

4. **Lack of individualized treatment:** The lawsuit argued that AMHI was not providing residents with individualized treatment plans that addressed their specific needs.

5. **Failure to provide adequate training:** The lawsuit alleged that AMHI was not providing adequate training to its staff on how to care for individuals with mental illness.

6. **Failure to provide access to necessary services:** The lawsuit claimed that AMHI was not providing residents with access to necessary services, such as psychological counseling, medical treatment, medication management, and social support services.

7. **Failure to protect residents from harm**: The lawsuit alleged that AMHI was not taking adequate steps to protect residents from harm, including from self-harm and abuse by other residents or staff.

8. **"Get along, go along" attitude.** Representatives of public guardianship, for residents in the hospital, were accused of having a 'get along, go along' attitude; they were not advocating public wards.

These claims were based on the experiences of numerous AMHI residents who had suffered from the alleged substandard care and treatment. The lawsuit sought to hold the State of Maine accountable for its failure to provide adequate care for individuals with mental illness and to reform the mental health system in Maine.

The AMHI Consent Decree was signed between the State of Maine and Disability Rights Maine (DRM) on August 2, 1990. It required the state to revamp the mental health system and provide specific services to those protected under the decree, such as priority on waitlists for placements. In 2004, AMHI changed its name to Riverview Psychiatric Center (RPC), and even though the hospital relocated, and changed its name, the state and the hospital are still bound by the decree. Additionally, the Maine Department of Health and Human Services (DHHS) was assigned to oversee the hospital. In 1995, a court master was assigned by the court, to oversee state compliance with the decree. The decree is still in place today.

The most important thing to remember about the decree is that anyone who was admitted to RPC on or after January 1, 1988, is a 'class member', is tracked by the state, and has a specific set of treatment rights established under the decree:

- **The right to receive treatment in the least restrictive environment:** This means that class members should be treated in the community whenever possible, rather than in a hospital or other institutional setting.

- **The right to participate in treatment planning:** Class members have the right to be involved in developing their own treatment plans. This includes the right to review and approve their treatment plans, as well as the right to request changes to their plans.

- **The right to be informed about their rights:** Class members have the right to be informed of their rights under the consent decree. This includes the right to receive information about their treatment options, as well as the right to file a complaint if they believe that their rights have been violated.

- **The right to be free from abuse and neglect:** Class members have the right to be treated with respect and dignity. This includes the right to be free from physical abuse, sexual abuse, and verbal abuse.

- **The right to confidentiality:** Class members' medical records are confidential. This means that their records will not be released without their consent.

In addition to these specific rights, the consent decree also requires the Maine Department of Health and Human Services (DHHS) to make several systemic changes to improve the quality of mental health care in Maine. These changes include:

- **Increasing the availability of community-based mental health services:** DHHS is required to increase the availability of community-based mental health services so that class members can receive treatment in their own homes and communities.

- **Improving the quality of care at Riverview Psychiatric Center:** DHHS is required to improve the quality of care at Riverview Psychiatric Center and in the community. This means that all providers, whether they are employees of the state or not, who receive state funds, are obligated to follow the requirements in the AMHI Consent Decree.

- **Ensuring that clients are involved in all aspects of the mental health system:** DHHS is required to ensure that clients are involved in all aspects of planning, developing, and implementing mental health services.

In 2023, the Maine Legislature approved a plan to end the AMHI Consent Decree, which had been in effect for over three decades. This decision was based on the belief that the state had made significant progress in reforming its mental health system and that the decree was no longer necessary; however, DRM and other advocates for individuals with mental illness have expressed concern about the potential impact of ending the decree. They argue that the state should continue to monitor and enforce the standards outlined in the decree to ensure that the mental health system remains responsive to the needs of Maine residents and recipients of care.

The AMHI Consent Decree is a landmark agreement that has significantly improved the lives of people with mental illness in Maine. The decree has helped to ensure that class members receive the treatment they need and deserve, and it has also helped to improve the overall quality of mental health care in the state. To learn more, visit: https://www.youtube.com/watch?v=40qCO_jrO7g&t=59s

Sonder vs. Brennan

The Eastern Maine Insane Hospital, one of two of Maine's psychiatric hospitals, also known as the Bangor Mental Health Institute, and now named the Dorothea Dix Psychiatric Center, has a long history, and played a prominent role in shaping the mental health field in Maine. The hospital was opened in 1901. The philosophy of the hospital was that it was a community and that everyone participated in those tasks that kept the hospital operating; ultimately contributing to the hospital's self-sufficiency. Clients worked in fields, raised livestock, worked in the kitchen, etc., until 1973, when a case of Sonder vs. Brennan determined that those working in public institutions, who are recipients of services, must be paid. This philosophy has been generalized to mental health and SUD agencies to mean that clients at their facilities, who are working are also paid. An example might be a client who serves on an all-voluntary board; in this example, the client must be paid for their work.

The bottom line is that anyone who works for an organization providing mental health and SUD services, and who receives services themselves, must be paid. Unfortunately, when running an all-voluntary program, it may be impossible to know who is receiving services and who is not due to confidentiality laws; therefore, it is best, if an organization is delivering mental health and SUD services, and when volunteers are benefiting the organization, those volunteers are paid, in compliance with labor laws.

Affordable Care Act of 2010

After years of pilot programs, on March 23, 2010, President Barrack Obama signed the Affordable Care Act (ACA) into law. The law has demonstrated savings in the medical and behavioral health field, which has defeated opposing arguments to the law since it was passed. In the mental health and SUD field, the law directed focus on what it referred to as the 'Triple Aim': Increased Quality, Increased Availability, and Decreased Costs.

The law also required electronic medical records (EMR) systems that had interagency operability (connected to other providers). The idea was that this would reduce costs if providers could communicate with each other, over an EMR, in real-time as services were being delivered. HealthInfoNet, in Portland, Maine, facilitated this process for the state, by creating a general release, known as 'Opt-In' or 'Opt-Out', which allowed providers to communicate how a client directs. It also invalidated the need for individual releases; however, some state agencies are still enforcing the antiquated rule requiring physical releases to be on record and updated every year.

To comply with the Triple Aim and the EMR requirement, Maine created a Behavioral Health Home (BHH) program. The program is known as Section 92, of the Maine Care Benefits Manual. The BHH program is not a place or a thing; it is case management with a focus on medical care. It also shifts the traditional fee-for-service (FFS) reimbursement rate for case management to a per-member-per-month (PMPM) rate. There are specific requirements to bill the rate; however, the general idea is that the fixed monthly reimbursement rate for the lower level of services to the majority of the BHH clients will cover the cost of service delivery to the lower amount of higher users of BHH services. When this program is operated correctly, it saves organizations, Medicaid, and insurance companies money; ultimately, saving taxpayers money. As a side note, one ethical dilemma with a fee-for-service model, such as mental case management, is that there is a tendency to provide more service than what is needed. The BHH model eliminates that dilemma.

Under the BHH model, the state also provides access to its billing analytics in the billing portal, known as HealthPAS. This billing data can provide insight into client treatment that is not captured by the EMR/HealthInfoNet. However, when both are used together, they are very powerful in painting a detailed picture of client history.

In Maine, and as a result of the Affordable Care Act, terms such as 'mental health', 'substance use', etc., have become known as behavioral health, collectively. This is also evidenced by state department reorganization (DHHS offices, the Office of Adult Mental Health and the Office of Substance Abuse, have merged and are now the Office of Behavioral Health). We see this change in community organizations also, such as Maine Mental Health Partners which changed their name, in 2013, to Maine Behavioral Healthcare; Maine Behavioral Health Organization took their name from the Affordable Care Act in 2011; Maine Behavioral Health Foundation (was designed to distribute grant funds to qualifying behavioral health agencies), etc.

Unfortunately, behavioral health terminology is oftentimes confused with retardation, intellectual disability, etc., which has also been known as behavioral health. Both categories of disability are very different; therefore, the context in which it is used is very important when using behavioral health terminology.

Maine Care Benefits Manual

The Maine Care Benefits Manual (MCBM) is a well-written insurance policy. It is the state's version of the Medicaid supplement. The manual can be found by googling, 'Maine Care Benefits Manual'. The manual is broken down into three chapters: Chapter I is the administrative part, that all organizations who are billing must follow; Chapter II is the program descriptions, which covers physician services to behavioral health homes; Chapter III looks a lot like Chapter II the way it is laid out, and it covers reimbursement rates.

It is very important to read Chapter I, and to understand what it says. And it is important to also read the respective section of Chapter II; for example, if you are delivering mental health case management, you should read Chapter II, Section 17, Community Support Services. Delivering services, without understanding the regulation, puts you and your agency at risk of repaying the billing, loss of license, and possibly a referral to the Attorney General's Office, Health Crimes Unit.

Current Landscape (2000s-Present)

In recent decades, Maine has continued to work to improve access to mental health services and promote recovery-oriented care. The state has developed a comprehensive network of community mental health centers and has made efforts to integrate mental health services into primary care settings. There is also a growing emphasis on providing peer support and other community-based resources to individuals with mental illness.

The evolution of psychiatric treatment in Maine has been marked by both progress and challenges. While new treatment methods and community-based care have improved the lives of many individuals, there is still a need to address stigma, ensure equitable access to care, and support ongoing recovery efforts.

Conclusion

Maine largely followed national trends on behavioral health treatment. Practices changed with an evolving understanding of mental illness and new approaches. In the 1970s, successful deinstitutionalization led to unintended consequences like homelessness and increased risks for patients. State psychiatric hospitals remained open, but faced accusations of inadequate staffing, unnecessary hospitalization, excessive restraint, lack of individual treatment, and insufficient services. These concerns led to a class-action lawsuit against the state; resulting in close monitoring of the mental health community. Recognition of co-occurring mental illness and substance use disorders (dual diagnosis) emerged in the late 1980s and was adopted by Maine in the 1990s. Co-occurring disorders pose significant risks and require integrated treatment, which became mandatory in Maine.

3. The Rules

Introduction

Promulgating rules serves multiple purposes, acting like a multifaceted tool in the government's toolbox. Firstly, it bridges the gap between broad laws and their practical application, translating legal principles into concrete actions and standards. This clarifies expectations for everyone involved, promoting fairness and consistency. Secondly, it allows for swift adaptation to ever-changing landscapes, addressing evolving needs and tackling unforeseen challenges without waiting for lengthy legislative processes. Thirdly, it safeguards the public by establishing minimum standards for health, safety, and welfare across various sectors, protecting individuals and businesses from harmful practices. Fourthly, it promotes efficiency and transparency in government operations, streamlining procedures and ensuring decisions are made based on established guidelines. Finally, it fosters accountability and public participation by allowing for input and scrutiny during the rulemaking process, ensuring that rules reflect the values and needs of the communities they serve. In essence, promulgating rules is about striking a balance between flexibility and order, ensuring a dynamic yet stable framework for governance.

Main Points and Procedure

The process for promulgating mental health rules in Maine is governed by the Maine Administrative Procedure Act (APA), which outlines the steps state agencies must follow when creating or changing rules. Here's a breakdown of the key stages:

1. Initiation:

- The Department of Health and Human Services (DHHS), identifies a need for a new rule or changes to an existing one. This could be driven by legislative mandates, stakeholder feedback, or other factors.
- DHHS drafts a proposed rule based on relevant laws, existing rules, and best practices.

2. Public Notice and Comment:

- DHHS publishes a notice of rulemaking in the Maine State Register, on the DHHS website, and in local newspapers. This notice includes information about the proposed rule, such as its purpose, summary, and where to find the full text.
- DHHS holds a public hearing to receive comments on the proposed rule. Anyone can attend and provide written or oral testimony.
- DHHS reviews all submitted comments and may revise the proposed rule based on the feedback received.

3. Legislative Review:

- DHHS submits the final proposed rule to the respective Joint Standing Committee and other relevant legislative committees for review.
- The committees may hold public hearings or request additional information from the DHHS.
- The committees issue a report recommending approval, disapproval, or amendments to the proposed rule.

4. *Agency Action:*

- DHHS considers the legislative committees' recommendations and any public comments received.

- DHHS makes a final decision on whether to adopt the proposed rule as is, modify it, or withdraw it.

- If DHHS adopts the rule, it is filed with the Secretary of State and made available on the Secretary of State's website. The effective date of the rule is typically stated within the rule itself.

The specific details of the rulemaking process may vary depending on the nature of the proposed rule. Some rules may be considered 'emergency rules' and can be implemented more quickly without following the full APA procedure. There are also legal provisions for challenging the validity of adopted rules.

Protocol for accessing rules from the Secretary of State

DO NOT ACCESS the rules from the Department of Health and Human Services (DHHS) website; it is the responsibility of the Secretary of State to ensure rules are up to date.

1. Go to the Maine Secretary of State website at https://www.maine.gov/sos/

2. Select the 'Corporations, Elections & Commissions' tab

3. Select 'State Rulemaking'

4. Select 'Rules by Department'

5. Select 'Health & Human Services'

6. Select '14-118 Office of Substance Abuse and Mental Health Services' for Substance Use Disorder Agency Licensing Rules, or '14-193 Office of Adult Mental Health' for Mental Health Agency Licensing Rules. In this example, we are going to select '14-118 Office of Substance Abuse and Mental Health Services'

State of Maine

Rule Chapters for the Department of Health and Human Services

Chapters available for downloading are highlighted. All chapters for this Department are formatted in Microsoft Word.

WARNING: While we have taken care with the accuracy of the files accessible here, they are not "official" state rules in the sense that they can be used before a court. Anyone who needs a

We also offer advice if you're having trouble trying to view these chapters.

10-144	Department of Health and Human Services - General
10-146	Office of Data Research and Vital Statistics
10-148	Office of Child and Family Services (OCFS), *part 1 (see also 14-472)*
10-149	Office of Aging and Disability Services, *part 1*
14-118	Office of Substance Abuse and Mental Health Services
14-191	Mental Health and Mental Retardation - General
14-193	Office of Adult Mental Health
14-197	Office of Aging and Disability Services, *part 2*
14-472	Office of Child and Family Services, *part 2 (the part that was formerly Bureau of Children with Special Needs; see also 10-148)*

7. In this example, we are interested in 'Ch. 5 Regulations for Licensing and Certifying of Substance Abuse Treatment Programs'. Once you click on the link below, it will download the regulation to your computer.

14 118	**Office of Substance Abuse and Mental Health Services (SAMHS)**
Ch. 1	Rules Governing Grants and Purchase of Service Agreements
Ch. 2	Driver Education and Evaluation Programs Procedure Manual
Ch. 3	Request for Proposal Policies
Ch. 5	Regulations for Licensing and Certifying of Substance Abuse Treatment Programs
Ch. 6	Regulations for Employee Assistance Programs for Employers Operating in the State of Maine
Ch. 11	Rules Governing the Controlled Substances Prescription Monitoring Program and Prescription of Opioid Medications
Ch. 18	Rules for Licensure of Residential Child Care Facilities *(repealed; see 10-144 ch. 36)*
Ch. 19	Rules Governing Community-Based Overdose Prevention Programs

8. To review the mental health licensing rules, go to Step 6, and instead of clicking on 14-118, click on '14-193 Office of Adult Mental Health' (which also includes the licensing of mental health services and facilities for children), and then on the next screen, select 'Ch. 6 Licensing of Mental Health Facilities'. The regulation will automatically download.

14 193	**Office of Adult Mental Health** *(formerly Bureau of Mental Health)*
Ch. 1	Rights of Recipients of Mental Health Services
Ch. 4	Rules for Board Representation at Community Mental Health Programs
Ch. 6	Licensing of Mental Health Facilities
Ch. 6A	Licensing of Mental Health Facilities: PNMI
Ch. 7	Rules Governing the Disclosure of Information Pertaining to Mentally Disables Clients
Ch. 18	Rules for the Licensure of Residential Child Care Facilities *(repealed; see 10-144 ch. 36)*
Ch. 20	Rules Governing the Disclosure of Limited Information Pertaining to Individuals Who Died in
Ch. 40	Review of Requests for Specialized Out-of-State Mental Health Treatment for Adults

Note: The first step to getting your organization licensed is to apply for licensure, using these regulations, through the Division of Licensing and Certification; then to provide services, you will need to have a contract with the respective DHHS office, either the Office of Behavioral Health (OBH) or the Office of Child and Family Services (OCFS).

To write a policy for licensing, visit the rules, and start from the beginning, by writing down each rule, and responding to it, as your policy. Give each rule its own page, so that it can be added to in the future, for example, updates for rules 1, 7 and 16 will be 1.1, 7.1, and 16.1. By giving each rule its own page, it will be easier to manage as there are updates. Do this for program policies also, obtained from the MaineCare Benefits Manual, Chapter II, Section 17 Community Integration (case management); copy each rule, to a single page, and respond to each one as your program policy.

The following is a mental health and substance use disorder (co-occurring, when combined), that was created from the rules. Students, providers, and faculty may use this assessment or any version of this assessment.

Comprehensive Assessment

Demographics

Name: Date:

Physical Address:

Phone Number:

Date of Birth:

Age:

Social Security Number:

Gender:

Military Status:

Guardian:

       Guardian Name:

       Guardian Address:

       Guardian Phone Number:

Emergency Contact:

       Emergency Contact Name:

       Emergency Contact Address:

Emergency Contact Phone Number:

Class Member:

Mental Health Advance Directive on File:

If not, the reason:

Was a Mental Health Advance Directive Offered:

Was there a crisis intervention in the last year?

Is there a potential for crisis in the future?

Is there a crisis or wellness plan on file?

Service Need & Support

Orientation: __Person __Place __Time __Situation __Disoriented

Speech: __WNL __Low __Loud __Mumbled __Slurred __Rapid __Pressured

Eye Contact: __WNL __Avoiding __Staring __Tracking __Wandering __Fleeting

Appearance: __Clean/Groomed __Disheveled __Unkempt __Severe Deficit

Describe Appearance:

Motor Activity: __WNL __Lethargic __Psychomotor Agitation

__Psychomotor Retardation __Tics __Tardive Dyskinesia __Altered Gait __Falls:

Describe Motor Activity:

Energy Level: __WNL __Increased __Decreased __Variable __Vegetive

Sleep: __WNL __Increased __Decreased __Variable __Interrupted

Appetite: __WNL __Increased __Decreased __Variable

Libido: __ Not Evaluated __WNL __Increased __Decreased __Variable __No Interest

Memory: __WNL __Impaired

Concentration: __WNL __Increased __Decreased __Easily Distracted

Cognition: __WNL __Mild __Moderate __Severe

Potentially dangerous variables:

History supporting a request for services:

Strengths and weaknesses relative to treatment:

Leisure, social, or recreational interests:

Family and support system's perception of needs for services:

Previous history of outpatient services:

Previous psychiatric hospitalization (starting with most recent; include dates):

Previous medical hospitalization:

Crisis intervention:

History of suicidal or homicidal behavior:

Family history of mental illness or suicide:

Diagnosis

Mental Health Diagnosis:

Diagnosis codes and descriptions:

Therapist: Date:

Agency:

Other (LOCUS, CANS, ANSA)

Name: Rater ID: Date:

If a therapist has not been identified, is one needed?

If one has been identified, who?

Agency:

How long have these services been provided?

Is there a psychiatrist involved?

If one has been identified, who?

Agency:

How long have these services been provided?

Current Mental Health Status

__**Mood:** __WNL __Sad/Depressed __Angry Irritable __Manic __Hypomanic __N/A

Other assessments of mood:

__**Affect:** __Full Range __Restricted __Flat __Labile __Tearful __Blunted __N/A

Is the affect congruent with mood?

Behavioral presentation: __Cooperative __Uncooperative __Engaging

__Withdrawn __Passive __Threatening__ Domineering __N/A

Other assessments of affect:

__**Through Process:** __WNL __Confused __Flight of Ideas __Distracted __

__Perseveration __Loose Associations __Circumstantial __Tangential

__Rumination __Other:

__**Thought Interference:** __None __Thought Insertion __Persecutory __Obsessive

__Compulsive __Other:

__**Hallucinations:** __None __Visual __Auditory __Tactile __Olfactory __Gustatory

__Command

Describe Hallucinations:

__**Delusions:** __None __Bizarre __Non-Bizarre __Paranoid __Religious __Persecutory

__Grandiose

Describe Delusions:

__**Orientated** (refer to Service Need & Support section): __Yes __No

Trauma & Abuse

__Abuse: __None __Sexual __Emotional __Neglect __Rape

Was abuse ever reported? __Yes __No

If 'Yes', to whom, and when?

Additional information:

__Domestic Violence: __None __Past __Present

    If present, is help desired?

    Perpetrator of domestic violence:

    Describe domestic violence:

    Flashbacks:

    Additional Information:

Substance Use and Abuse

History of substance use and abuse:

Past substance use disorder treatment (when, where, program):

Current substance use (type, duration, pattern, frequency, other pertinent information):

Seeking treatment for substance use disorders: __Yes __No __Undecided

    If yes, from what:

Stages of Change: __Relapse __Pre-contemplation __Contemplation __Determination

    __Action __Maintenance

If sober, how long?

    What are risk factors for relapse?

Medical Conditions & History

Primary Care Physician: __Yes __No Doctor's Name:

      Practice:

      Other current medical providers:

Current Medical Conditions:

Past Medical Conditions:

Allergies: __No __Yes

      If yes, list:

Has a neurological assessment ever been completed?

Is there a history of brain injury? __No __Yes

      If yes, when, how, and was there any previous treatment?

Nutritional Assessment? __Needed __Requested __N/A

Family history of medical issues:

Dentist: __Yes __No Doctor's Name:

      Practice:

      Current Dental Assessment and Conditions: __N/A __Assessment Needed

Medications

Medication Name	Prescriber	Frequency	Dose

Past Medication Taken:

Medication Name	Prescriber	Frequency	Dose

Other pertinent medical information:

Familial History & Childhood Development

Birthplace:

Parent's Marital Status: __N/A __Married __Divorced __Separated

Father's Name:

     If alive, where does he reside?

Relationship dynamics:

If deceased, when and cause?

Mother's Name:

     If alive, where does she reside?

Relationship dynamics:

If deceased, when and cause?

Siblings (List in birth order):

Describe relationships with siblings:

Assessment of developmental milestones:

Describe significant childhood events:

Additional sources of support:

Social History

Marital Status:

Marital History:

Personal relationships assessment:

Children and ages:

If children are underage, where do they reside?

Spiritual/Religion

Religious Preference:

Spiritual Beliefs:

Environment/Housing/Financial

Rent Subsidy: __Yes __No If 'Yes', What kind?

Section 8: __Yes __No If pending, date of application:

Sources of Income: __SSDI __SSI/Survivor __SSI/SSDI __TANF __General Assistance

   __Other:

Pending Social Security case: __Yes __No __N/A

   If Yes, date applied for?

Lawyer?

Transportation Used: __MaineCare funded __Public __Own __Other __N/A

Driver's License: __Yes __No

State ID Card: __Yes __No __Needed?

Summary/Narrative

Person completing assessment:

Credentials:

Signature:

Date:

Clinician:

Credentials:

Signature:

Date:

Conclusion

Promulgating rules play a crucial role in effective governance, bridging the gap between broad laws and their practical application. By translating legal principles into concrete actions, rules clarify expectations, ensure fairness, and adapt to changing needs. They safeguard public well-being by establishing safety standards and promote transparency and efficiency in government functioning. Finally, they foster accountability by allowing public participation in the rulemaking process.

4. Completing the Assessment

Introduction

A mental health assessment is the first step to determining what type of care a client needs. It involves talking with the client and asking about their history and their current symptoms. Providers will also need to ask about family and social history, as well as substance use habits. It is the best practice to get a records release for the most recent physical examination or make a referral for one. This is to rule out any physical conditions that may produce symptoms that mimic the effects of mental disorders. For example, a neurological condition, thyroid disease, or autoimmune disorder could all have symptoms that mimic those of a mental illness.

A good provider or assessor will consider a client's gender and cultural background when interpreting the results of their assessments. It is important for the provider to also be aware of their own biases as the assessment progresses and to seek supervision if they are unable to continue the assessment because of their biases.

Assessment and screening tools help to identify high-risk individuals who may benefit from brief intervention and referral to treatment. Those identified as needing more extensive assessment and treatment are referred to mental health or drug abuse specialists for follow-up treatment, such as a Licensed Clinical Social Worker (LCSW), a Licensed Alcohol and Drug Counselor (LADC), or both. A comprehensive assessment requires a thorough review of a client's family, social, and sexual relationships; and medical, psychological, and substance abuse histories.

The assessment form in this book was created from the rules and templates from a multimillion-dollar non-profit mental health organization that I built and directed for about 10 years; the assessment has been adopted by providers, audited by the state and federal government, and recommended to other agencies. The assessment complies with state and federal auditing standards.

Main Points

Demographics

The beginning portion of the mental health assessment, 'Demographics', is straightforward. If the client has a guardian, then the assessment should be completed with the guardian's permission, or with the guardian present. It is also important to note if the individual is a class member, or a class member public ward, as they receive special consideration under the AMHI Consent Decree. **Anyone who was admitted to RPC on or after January 1, 1988, is a 'class member'.**

It is also important to note whether the client has any advanced directives, such as a mental health advanced directive, medical directives, do not resuscitate orders, etc. If the client does not have any advanced directives, they should be offered one to be filled out on their own. Unfortunately, there may be some liability in directing clients how to complete advanced directives; therefore, they should seek assistance from a family member or an attorney. If they have a directive, it will be important to document it in the assessment and file it in the treatment record. If the client declines the directive, the client should sign a document stating that it was declined, for record auditing purposes. The form can state something as simple as, "I, _____ have declined to establish a Mental Health Advanced Directive with [insert Agency] at this time", with a date and signature block for the client, and the assessor as a witness.

Service Need & Support

In the Service Need & Support section, the first question is the mental status exam. I like to conduct the mental status exam in casual conversation; for example, I can never remember the date, so I will ask the client for the date, ask them what their name is, etc. Sometimes I might ask for a specific address, and then ask for a more general address. I might also ask them if they know why I am meeting with them, to see if they are oriented to the situation. Many of the other questions in this section are important in identifying symptomologies for diagnosing.

Many case managers and providers feel uncomfortable when assessing the libido of their clients. Additionally, the client may also feel uncomfortable. There may be times when assessing libido may be culturally unacceptable. For example, in most scenarios, it is inappropriate for males to assess libido. For example, a male assessor who is open about his heterosexuality may not be appropriate for our clients who are not heterosexual. In my opinion, in most scenarios, it is inappropriate for a male to assess the libido of a female client, especially if they are both close in age. In some instances, it may also be inappropriate for a female to assess another female's libido. The libido question is almost always best for the therapist to explore in session. Therefore a 'not-evaluated' block has been added and should be used in most cases.

In the 'Potentially dangerous variables' area, it is important to note the environmental variables that may contribute to harming the client. For example, frequent falls should be noted, leaving the stove on should be noted, access to guns should be noted, etc. In this area, variables that exacerbate the situation should be identified. In the 'History supporting a request for services' area, a history of services should be noted. It is important to show a trend in this area. **A trend is three or more occurrences** of an incident, for example, three hospitalizations. Two occurrences are not a trend because if the occurrences were data, they could not be plotted on a graph with a trend line; there must be at least three points on a graph to draw a trend line. In this area, it is also appropriate to note any history of diagnoses.

In the 'Strengths and weaknesses relative to treatment' area, it is important to discuss trends of treatment failures so that they are not repeated, and strengths or what has worked well, so that they can be capitalized on in crisis planning and treatment. The strengths and weaknesses should also be reflected in the individual support plan. Likewise, the 'Leisure, social, or recreational interests' are for the same purposes.

In the 'Family and support system's perception of needs for services' area, the family should be engaged if possible. In some instances, it may be appropriate to ask the client what they believe their family's perception of their needs is. Unfortunately, when clients get to the point where they need intensive care such as mental health case management, they have damaged or lost the relationships with their family. It is not uncommon for clients to not have any family involved in the care. This should not mean that the assessor should not attempt to engage the family. The family can be one of the greatest sources of support when they are involved in treatment. Family contact information is requested in the demographics portion of the assessment.

In the 'Previous history of outpatient services' area, list histories such as case management services, counseling services, and intensive outpatient services. These histories should be listed starting with the most recent date. The next two questions, 'previous history of outpatient services' and 'previous psychiatric hospitalization', should be completed the same way.

In the 'Crisis intervention' area, it will be important to note any crisis interventions that have occurred in the past in the same way the previous questions were addressed. In this area, it should be determined if there is a need for ongoing crisis intervention. If there is a need for ongoing crisis intervention, there should be consideration of a crisis alert. A crisis alert is where the local crisis agency is notified of the potential of a crisis. A release of information should be obtained before submitting a crisis alert. Each crisis agency may have its protocols on how it would like crisis alerts to be submitted. It's best to contact them ahead of time, to find out what their process is.

The next section intends to determine suicidal ideation. When I was a social worker for the state, I assessed suicide on the following: expressed willingness to complete suicide; history of suicide attempts; plan to commit suicide, such as a violent plan or a plan to do it after a party to say goodbye to friends; access to lethal objects such as knives or firearms; and willingness to contract for safety. The research does not seem definitive on whether contracting for safety is effective, but I always did it anyway in case it did work. One of the best ways to assess for suicide is to simply ask the individual if they are suicidal (expressed willingness). I found that individuals who are contemplating suicide are honest about it. Unfortunately, the risk factors are not easy to identify when someone is contemplating suicide and are often more obvious once someone has completed suicide. If the client does have suicidal ideation, the assessment should continue as a crisis assessment, and the client's safety should be managed. A family history can also help determine the risk for mental illness, substance use disorders, and suicide.

Whenever anyone states they are having suicidal ideation or thinking about completing suicide, it is time to act. **All threats of suicide should be taken seriously.**

Diagnosis

The diagnostic section of the assessment is a complex area. Portions of the diagnostic section may be completed by various providers. Generally, case managers screen for qualification of services whereas the clinician or therapist completes a diagnostic assessment and attaches it to the assessment. Some assessments have areas for the clinician to enter their diagnostic information on the assessment forms directly. The three main assessments to be concerned with are LOCUS, CANS, and ANSA. The following is a brief description of each:

LOCUS:

- Stands for Level of Care Utilization System.

- It's a statewide assessment tool used to determine the appropriate level of care for individuals requiring mental health services in Maine.

- The LOCUS assessment considers factors like symptom severity, risk of harm to self or others, functional abilities, and support needs.

- Based on the assessment results, individuals are placed on a continuum of care ranging from outpatient services to inpatient hospitalization.

CANS:

- Stands for Child and Adolescent Needs and Strengths.

- It's a standardized assessment tool specifically designed for evaluating the mental health needs of children and adolescents aged 5-18 years.

- Similar to LOCUS, CANS assesses various aspects like emotional and behavioral symptoms, social and family functioning, and academic performance.

- Based on the CANS assessment, individualized treatment plans and service recommendations are developed for each child or adolescent.

ANSA:

- Stands for Adult Needs and Strengths Assessment.

- Similar to CANS, it's a standardized assessment tool used to evaluate the mental health needs of adults aged 19 and above.

- ANSA assesses areas like psychiatric symptoms, cognitive abilities, daily living skills, and social supports.

- Based on the ANSA assessment, appropriate treatment and service recommendations are made for each adult seeking mental health services.

All three of these assessments, the LOCUS, CANS, and ANSA, are standardized tools used in Maine's mental health system to determine the appropriate level of care for individuals based on their specific needs and strengths. These assessments play a crucial role in ensuring individuals receive the most effective and appropriate mental health and substance use disorders services possible. To be able to use these screens providers must be trained. To receive training on these screenings, providers will need to contact the Maine Department of Health and Human Services.

If a therapist has not been identified then one will need to be identified, at the very least, to assess the client for a mental health and or substance use disorder diagnosis for determination of qualification for services. Additionally, a psychiatric provider should be identified if needed.

In Maine, mental health and substance use disorder clinicians are required to complete a diagnostic form. This form is normally referred to as a clinical eligibility opinion or verification form. The form should have basic demographic information, the service requested, and whether the individual is a class member. The form should state something to the effect of, "The above member meets the eligibility criteria as outlined in the current published version of Maine Care Benefits, based on documented or reported history, where s/he is likely to have future episodes, related to mental illness, with a non-excluded DSM-5 diagnosis, that would result in or have significant risk factors of homelessness, criminal justice involvement or require a mental health inpatient treatment greater than 72 hours, or residential treatment unless community support program services are provided; based on documented or reported history. My opinion is that the member has a strong likelihood of becoming: [then state for the following reasons: homeless, hospitalized, involved with the criminal justice system, or placed in residential treatment]". On the form, it should be noted how the opinion was obtained: documented history, reported history, as the treating clinician/doctor, and screening for service tool and score. Additionally, the report must note how the clinical history was obtained: Oral history obtained from the client, oral history obtained from a provider, written history obtained from the client, or written history obtained from a provider. Lastly, the form must include a brief discussion. The following is an example:

> *Mike is a 35-year-old Caucasian male who comes from a family that has a history of depression, PTSD, and substance abuse. Mike reported that he has a history of schizoaffective disorder, bipolar, PTSD, and Depression. He stated that as a child, he*

was a victim of physical and emotional abuse by his biological father, as well as verbal and emotional abuse by his mother. Mike discussed that he may have had therapy with his parents as a child, according to his mother, but does not remember it. Mike says that as an adult he was physically, sexually, and verbally abused. He says that he tried to report the abuse, but those he reported it to seemed to be involved with the authorities or were the authorities. When asked to elaborate, he hesitated and stated that while he was in the military, from 2000 to 2002, he was a victim of physical, verbal, and racial abuse. Mike said that his first sergeant was African American who created a hostile work environment. He remarked that on one occasion, a superior to the first sergeant witnessed racial comments, by the first sergeant, and took disciplinary action against the first sergeant. Mike reported that this led to unbearable treatment by the first sergeant, and he used drugs to cope and was positive for marijuana on urine analyses; after returning from being absent without leave. He said that he eventually received an honorable discharge. Mike stated that any hard drugs he used started while he was in the military, with a history of stimulant and opiate use, and that he quit using drugs when he had a son. Mike later stated that he had been on and off drugs, since his son was born, with the last use being in 2022; in June of 2022, he said he overdosed on heroin. Mike says for medical issues, he has high blood pressure and cholesterol. Mike reported that in 2022 he had a stroke but is unable to articulate the medical details around it. He says that he has brain damage but does not seem to present as a TBI client. He does not recall having a neurological exam. Mike reported that he smokes up to one pack of cigarettes a day but has been trying to cut back and can go about two and a half days with one pack. Mike stated that he was homeless in 2022 when he was using various drugs and that involvement with his parents contributed to his destabilization and hospital admissions. Mike says that he has a history of crisis incidents and psychiatric admissions, including admissions to Seton and Penobscot Bay Hospital, with the last admission being at the VA in July of 2023. He also reported being at Riverview Psychiatric Center where he was also prescribed

Seroquel. Mike says that contact with family destabilizes him and that he does not want any contact with them. Additionally, he remarked that both of his brothers have passed away. Mike says that he has hallucinations when he does not take his medications and currently takes Seroquel four times a day. He also remarked that he has difficulty getting to sleep and that he has nightmares and flashbacks regarding past experiences. He stated that a nightmare would ruin his entire day and that he wouldn't sleep. Mike says that one of his goals in treatment is to learn to trust others. According to the case management supervisor and executive director, when Mike did a walk-in on December 9, 2023, to self-refer, he was manic and grossly disorganized and was on the verge of crisis. Mike informed the supervisors that he did not know how he was going to make it through Christmas and that not having his brothers around made it that much harder. Mike reportedly has a history of wanting to hurt himself and reportedly attempted suicide in 2022. Mike is at risk for homelessness, psychiatric hospitalization, and harm to himself without support. He has no family or friends in the state of Maine, resulting in no personal support system available to help him. Given the information provided, Mike has a primary diagnosis of schizoaffective disorder bipolar type (F25.0) and Post Traumatic Stress Disorder (F43.10). Additionally, he has a secondary diagnosis of Opioid Use Disorder, Severe, Sustained Remission (F11.20) and Stimulant Use Disorder, Other/Unspecified, Severe, Sustained Remission (F15.20).

The summary should always include **medical necessity**, and either state or demonstrate, **marked** behavior. Medical necessity is the determination of whether a healthcare service or treatment is reasonable and necessary based on a client's specific condition, current accepted standards of medical practice, and expected health outcomes. It's the foundation of claims review, reimbursement, and processing. Insurers play a major role in determining medical necessity, and their decisions are often influenced by guidelines established by professional medical organizations or the Centers for Medicare & Medicaid Services. To be able to bill for a service, the assessor must show that the mental health condition causes or worsens a medical condition, to the likely point of increased need for services, without the current recommended treatment.

When using the DSM for assigning a diagnosis, it will be important to develop a crosswalk, to the ICD, for billing. The state's system only accepts ICD codes, however, for record keeping, clinicians are required to complete a DSM diagnosis for the assessment.

Current Mental Health Status

The next section in the assessment is the 'Current Mental Health Status' exam. This section is attempting to collect data on abnormal behavior. Some behaviors that are associated with abnormal behavior include changes in mood or behavior, changes in sleep or eating patterns, changes in thinking or perception, compulsive and obsessive behaviors, and suicidal thoughts or behaviors. Some of the disorders that are associated with these criteria are major depressive disorder, anxiety disorders, schizophrenia, and substance use disorders.

Trauma & Abuse

In the trauma and abuse section of the assessment information regarding the type of abuse and whether it was reported is collected. In Maine, providers are required to complete a mental health trauma and substance use disorder screening with their clients. The name of the form is AC/OK, created by Dr. Andrew Cherry, from Oklahoma. To learn more about the form please visit https://ccsme.org/wp-content/uploads/2017/02/AC-OK-Screening-tool.pdf.

Questions about domestic violence are also asked in this section. It is important to identify provider biases, and not provide personal commentary. It is possible that the client has developed an attachment to abusers, or identifies with them, and commenting on the perpetrators of violence, may also be offensive to the client. It is also important to keep in mind that the assessment intends to gather information to inform treatment. Questions and details should be surface level only and should not re-traumatize the client.

Substance Use and Abuse

The purpose of this section is to gather information on past substance abuse including when, where, and the agencies treatment was received at. Outpatient treatment and hospitalizations should be listed in order from the most recent admission. This section also gathers information on current substance use patterns.

The most important part of this section is determining where a client is in the stages of change. Stage change theory, also known as the Transtheoretical Model, is a widely used framework for understanding how people progress through behavior change, including addressing substance use disorders. It helps clinicians appropriately align treatment where clients are when they enter services. It proposes that individuals go through five distinct stages on their journey to overcoming or managing their substance use:

1. Precontemplation: This stage is characterized by a lack of awareness or concern about the negative consequences of substance use. Individuals may not be considering changing their behavior at all.

2. Contemplation: In this stage, individuals become aware of the problems associated with their substance use and start to consider changing their behavior. They may weigh the pros and cons of continuing their current behavior against the potential benefits of change.

3. Preparation: This stage involves actively planning and taking steps towards change. Individuals may start researching treatment options, gathering resources, and developing coping mechanisms.

4. Action: This stage is marked by the initiation of actual behavioral changes. Individuals may begin reducing or stopping their substance use, participating in treatment programs, and adopting healthier lifestyle habits.

5. Maintenance: This stage is about preventing relapse and maintaining the positive changes made in the action stage. Individuals learn to identify and manage triggers, practice self-care, and develop long-term support systems.

The key principles of stage change theory include:

- Change is a process, not a single event. It takes time and effort to move through the stages and achieve lasting change.

- People move through the stages at their own pace. There is no set timeline, and individuals may cycle back and forth between stages before reaching maintenance.

- Different interventions are appropriate for different stages. Treatment approaches should be tailored to the individual's current stage of change to be most effective.

In the context of substance use disorder treatment, stage change theory can be used to:

- Assess an individual's readiness to change. This can help treatment providers develop an appropriate treatment plan.

- Motivate individuals to act. By understanding the stages of change, individuals can see where they are in the process and feel more empowered to move forward.

- Develop targeted interventions. Specific strategies can be used to address the needs of individuals at different stages, increasing the likelihood of successful change.

Medical Conditions & History

Present and past medical conditions such as physical, neurological, nutritional, dental, and allergies are covered in this area. The most important thing to remember in this area is to make sure the medical conditions and medications are spelled correctly. Sometimes conditions and medications that are spelled similarly, may be very different. The State and federal government may also issue citations for these types of record errors.

Releases of information should be requested for all providers listed in this section.

Familial History & Childhood Development

Assessing familial history and childhood development in a mental health assessment and substance use disorder assessment is critically important for determining risk factors, through family history and adverse childhood experiences. Certain mental health conditions have a strong genetic component, meaning a family history of these conditions can increase an individual's risk of developing them. Knowing about family history helps to identify potential genetic vulnerabilities and tailor treatment accordingly. Dysfunctional family relationships, substance abuse within the family, and poor parenting practices can contribute to the development of mental health problems. Understanding family dynamics helps provide context for the individual's current situation and informs family-based interventions if needed.

Traumatic events, neglect, and abuse during childhood can significantly impact brain development and increase the risk of various mental health issues in adulthood. Early attachment experiences play a crucial role in emotional development and future relationships. Assessing attachment styles can help explain challenges with interpersonal relationships and inform therapeutic approaches focused on attachment repair.

When assessing developmental milestones, the provider should consider asking about special education and learning disabilities. Oftentimes, these are indicative of childhood trauma (including excessive yelling and spanking), mental health problems, and substance use and abuse. It is in this section that the provider should be able to formulate an ACEs score (adverse childhood experiences). The term ACEs is a term that is used to describe potentially traumatic events that occur in childhood, ages 0-17, and can have a lasting negative impact on a person's physical and mental health. The assessment considers exposure to violence, household dysfunction, neglect, and other events, that are linked to a wide range of mental health problems such as depression, anxiety, post-traumatic stress disorder, attention deficit hyperactivity disorder, eating disorders, substance use disorders, and suicide; and chronic physical health problems such as heart disease, stroke, cancer, diabetes, and chronic pain.

It is important to note that not everyone who experiences ACEs will develop mental health or physical health problems. ACEs do increase the risk, and the more ACEs a person experiences, the greater the risk. Studies have shown that about 61% of adults in the United States have experienced at least one ACE. Knowing about family history and childhood experiences can help rule out certain diagnoses and differentiate between possible contributing factors. This leads to a more accurate diagnosis and more effective treatment planning. To read more about ACEs, visit https://www.chcs. org/media/TA-Tool-Screening-for-ACEs-and-Trauma_020619.pdf

Social History

In the 'Social history' section, the client should be asked to assess their relationships.

Spiritual/Religion and Environment/Housing/Financial

These sections are straightforward. In the 'Environment/Housing/Financial', it will be important to assess whether the client has transportation. Additionally, this is a great place to document the client's MaineCare number, which will be needed for billing. If the client does not drive, then it may be important to get a state ID for the client. The ID card will be needed to apply for benefits and use certain insurance and MaineCare services.

Summary/Narrative

In the 'Summary/Narrative' section, all the pertinent information is summarized. The following are some examples:

Example 1.

> *Josh is a class member who was released into the community after a 9.5-year prison sentence for attempted murder. He is in the process of being transferred from the emergency room to an inpatient psychiatric facility. He carries a lengthy mental health diagnosis of psychosis, schizophrenia, depression, and anxiety according to the Intensive Case Manager (ICM) that he was meeting with at Maine State Prison.*

His updated diagnosis will be forthcoming. Josh is a 36-year-old male who has no natural support. He was released two days ago to the Trinity Shelter in Skowhegan. Due to his mental health issues, he was unable to stay there for more than 12 hours. He reports that other guys at the shelter were trying to kill him and that the food was poisoned. He left the shelter and went to the closest bridge where he contemplated suicide. He reports that he became disoriented and eventually two strangers pointed him in the direction of the hospital. Josh reports that before he got to the hospital, he had urinated in his pants due to his extreme level of anxiety. Crisis further describes Josh as being psychotic and afraid to go to sleep because "he fears waking up in the third dimension." Josh reports that as a child his father "used to hit me like I was a full-grown man." He states that he tolerated the abuse until he was 13 and then went to live with his biological mother who "dumped me at Acadia hospital when she found out I had a mental illness." Josh reports from there he went into DHHS custody. He reports that he frequently ran away and was on his own after the age of 13. He states, "It was very lonely." Josh reports witnessing his grandparents sexually abuse his sister. He states they were emotionally abusive toward him including calling him names and telling him he was worthless. Josh reports having multiple hospitalizations as a child and adult. Josh reports that in the past he has had ECT which has caused permanent memory impairment including not knowing times and dates. He became an AMHI class member during a four-month stay while he was on trial for attempted murder. He reports that he was angry and beat another guy with a barbell and stomped on him. Josh reports that he has six years of prison time hanging over his head and four years of probation. He states, "I have prison coping skills but I don't know how to deal out here." Josh reports that he has no family members to contact and no other natural support.

Example 2.

Client was born in 1977 in Queens New York and reports that he has met his developmental milestones on time. He stated that his ADHD has affected him and that later his substance abuse has also affected him. Client stated that he was in crisis last week and that he really begins to get upset when he thinks about the difficulty that he has looking for a place stay (he is currently staying with a friend). He stated that his status as a lifetime registrant gets him down and sometimes leads to crisis. He stated that he has been trying to fight this requirement. Client stated that he also has bipolar and PTSD. Client has a long history of being in and out of jail, and in 1997 escaped from a prison work detail when he only had 13 days left. Client stated that he struggles with substance abuse and is currently in treatment for it. He attends IOP, counseling, and also attends NA groups. Client stated that he is currently being treated with suboxone at Crisis and Counseling. Client stated that he does have some court dates that he will be required to attend because of some recent arrests, which include receiving stolen property and stealing a car. Client is hopeful that he will only get fined and that he will continue treatment. Client is also hopeful that case management will help him to explore resources that are available to him. 1. Calculation of LOCUS Composite Score I. Risk of Harm 3, II. Functional Status 3, III. Medical, Addictive and Psychiatric Co-Morbidity 3, IV Recovery Environment A. Level of Stress 3, B. Level of Support 3, V Treatment and Recovery History 3, VI Attitude and Engagement 3. Composite LOCUS Score (add numbers in right column) 21. 2. LOCUS-Derived Level of Care Recommendation: IV.

Example 3. Annual update from the year before:

Martin is a 52-year-old male from Augusta, presenting with Post-Traumatic Stress Disorder. Martin has lived with others for several years and has been taken advantage of by everyone he's lived with during that time. He has had difficulties with medication providers due to medications being stolen and has been unable to provide for his basic needs because his money was stolen as well. Martin recently moved into his own private apartment but reports being extremely bored and often depressed because living alone is difficult, though he feels being depressed and living alone is better than being taken advantage of.

Martin was enlisted in the military for approximately fifteen years as a scout sniper and served in multiple conflicts, including Panama, Grenada, and Desert Storm, and has over 70 confirmed kills. He describes his PTSD as coming from that time when "you take that shot you know you shouldn't, the shot you know means you have killed one too many people". Martin was discharged from the military honorably.

While enlisted he suffered an accident jumping from an aircraft that caused him to shatter both knees and several other bones and has had multiple surgeries on each. He was also hit by a truck while working for a construction company and broke his neck. He stated that he has shocked everyone by even being able to walk following his accidents. Martin now goes to Maine General Physiatry for pain medication, and without it, would be in debilitating pain.

One of the injuries Martin sustained was a brain injury that affected his frontal lobe. Martin has difficulty controlling feelings of anger and desires to do physical harm to others, but does maintain proper boundaries, and discusses these issues with his providers once he feels safe talking to them. Martin has been working with this writer for approximately seven months and feels comfortable discussing his issues with him, except those directly related to his trauma.

Martin struggles with change, and his ability to form relationships with people. He tried therapy several times in the past but reported that several therapists scheduled with him and never met him, a couple met him once or twice, and the longest someone saw him was about six weeks. The therapist encouraged him to open up and discuss his trauma history, and upon doing so, was unable to continue seeing him due to vicarious traumatization. Another therapist left her agency after seeing Martin a few times. Each time Martin receives a new provider without any warning, he enters a crisis state or becomes hospitalized. This writer's first meeting with Martin was when he picked him up from the behavioral health unit at the hospital because he was informed a week or two prior that this writer would be his new case manager.

As a result of Martin's trauma history, significant focus has been placed during his treatment on finding him stable situations to exist in that do not trigger him. Housing was the primary goal and has been met, and he is now beginning to openly discuss other needs that must be met, such as seeing a doctor for something other than pain and looking at social activities. Martin does not do well in large crowds due to his trauma but does desire to interact with other people which would be healthy for him to engage with.

Example 4. Updated Note/Running Note

On October 10, 2012, DHHS referred the client under the Transitional, Engagement, and Outreach grant. The client is currently homeless and left Florida to arrive in Augusta by bus on October 9, 2012. The client stated that she walked in on her boyfriend who was molesting her 12-year-old son. The client also came with her daughter. The client was staying with her mother but could not stay there because she did not know when her boyfriend was going to get out of jail and had DVs on him. The client is also a class member. She was put up by DHHS in Augusta. During her time in Maine, she has worked on her Maine Care, General Assistance, BRAP, and contacted numerous shelters: Bread of Life Ministries, Augusta 626-3479-Full, New Beginnings, Lewiston 795-4070-Children Only Hope Haven Gospel, Lewiston 790-4070, Adults Only St. Martin, Lewiston 786-4690, Full and do not take children Hope House, Bangor 217-6713, Does not take children New Hope for Woman, Solon, will only take mother and daughter but not son Bangor Area Homeless Shelter, 947-0092, Adults Only City of Portland Family Shelter 772-8339 Rockport Hospitality House, 592-1422, Left Message, no response Light House Shelter, Kids, 774-3164 Emmaus House, Ellsworth, 667-3962 Full, Put on Waiting List Tedford Shelter, full*******Present********Agency staff have assisted client with getting an apartment by using DHHS resources and by using General Assistance. The GA Director filed a CPS report against the client, stating to agency staff that the client was fleeing an open CPS case in Florida and that she came to*

Maine with a plan for homelessness. When agency staff was contacted by DHHS CPS, staff explained that she was fleeing her boyfriend, not knowing when he was going to get out of jail and that she has been maintaining contact with Florida DHS and the Attorney General's office to testify. The CPS worker met with the client and closed the case. Agency staff have also assisted the client with obtaining TANF and applying for Social Security disability. Agency staff assisted the client with enrolling her children in school and coordinating counseling. The client continues to be anxious and often expresses that she is overwhelmed, however, she stated that she works for her family no matter how discouraged she gets. The client has a history of suicidal ideation and has attempted suicide on five occasions. The client has stated that she has been hospitalized twice in Florida for suicide attempts, and when she was younger, was placed in AMHI (when she was eleven). The client is working on obtaining a job and has had several interviews. Agency staff will continue to support the client as her social security paperwork is processed, and if denied, will assist with an attorney, support the client as she looks for a job, and continue to work on outreach goals.

Example 5.

Ron is a 44-year-old white male who was recently released from the Maine Correctional Center after serving time for trafficking methamphetamines. Ron was born in California. His father was a Vietnam vet and was physically and verbally abusive. Ron does not perceive his parents' alcohol consumption as a problem, however, he had his first drink at 10 years of age and was encouraged to drink. Child protective services were involved, and at 12 years old, Ron left his home. Since that time, he has been in and out of jail. Ron says that every time he got in trouble with the law, alcohol was involved, except for his last charge. Ron says that he has built a tolerance for alcohol and at one point was able to consume a 30-pack of beer and a 1/5th of liquor a day. He maintains that he is not interested in other drugs and that alcohol is his preference. Ron says that alcohol, or 'Hootch', and drugs are available in the prison, and remarked that he did not know why, but he did not drink or use drugs. Additionally, he has been sober for about six weeks, since being released, for a total of 17 months of sobriety. Ron says there is not too much that bothers him these days, except that he is concerned that his mother is not doing well and it may trigger his drinking. Ron is required to attend substance abuse treatment as a condition of release. He says he has had treatment in the past and does not feel that he needs it now. Ron does however discuss that he has cravings and thinks about alcohol. His goals for treatment are to improve coping skills, stress management, improve problem-solving abilities, set priorities, and develop alternatives to alcohol use in high-risk situations. Ron's strengths are his ability to articulate himself clearly and a renewed commitment to stay sober. Follow-up care will include natural supports such as Alcoholics Anonymous.

After completing the narrative/summary section of the assessment, it will be important for the provider to sign the form and provide his or her credentials. One of the most common citations on behavioral health records is that the provider did not provide their credentials (**every time you sign or print your name on a behavioral health record, you are required to also provide your respective credentials**). Additionally, the form is required to be signed by the provider's clinical supervisor. The assessment is not considered complete until it has been reviewed by a clinical supervisor. Another common citation is that the providers did not date the signatures; all parts of the form must be completed.

Culture

An important component to assessment is the role that culture plays in it. Culture is the beliefs, behaviors, and attitudes of a group of people. Cultural competence refers to cultural knowledge, skills, and attitudes reflected in policies, practices, and procedures, that enable providers to interact effectively with individuals from diverse backgrounds. It focuses on developing an understanding of how disparities can be shaped by culture and on fostering a culturally responsive treatment environment.

Achieving cultural competence requires organizational commitment, training, and ongoing improvement. This includes ensuring that diversity is openly discussed throughout the organization and that the effects of culture are considered at every level. It also requires promoting treatment relationships where people are encouraged to discuss their culture and values with their providers.

This can be done by implementing culturally competent policies and procedures, providing staff with adequate cultural awareness and sensitivity training, and supporting and facilitating the development of peer supports, self-help groups and other community resources that are relevant to the individuals served. Research suggests that these factors are important to the successful delivery of services.

Providers must be cautious when assessing clients from cultures other than their own. This is because people from different cultures may present differently with mental health and substance use disorders. It is important to maintain cultural humility and respect clients' cultural beliefs and values. This helps avoid making assumptions about a client's culture based on stereotypes or ethnocentric values (that belong to the counselor's own culture).

Creating truly culturally responsive assessments means understanding that culture extends beyond clients' personal racial or ethnic background, into their local context, and history. It also includes a client's family, community, and school experience. A culturally responsive assessment allows the client to draw from their strengths and cultural fluencies when addressing treatment goals, instead of reinforcing dominant culture values and state-adopted content standards. This approach will help ensure that the assessment is relevant to the individual client's treatment needs.

Conclusion

A thorough mental health assessment, involving client interviews, history review, and physical health checks, helps determine appropriate care. Providers consider cultural background and biases while using screening tools to identify individuals needing brief interventions or referrals to specialists like LCSWs or LADCs. This comprehensive process, based on a proven organizational model, ensures clients receive the right support according to state and federal regulations.

5. Treatment Plan

Introduction

The treatment plan is informed by the assessment; without it, the plan is not valid, and agencies are cited when they are unable to produce an assessment in support of a treatment plan, during an audit. Treatment planning is about creating a customized and goal-oriented approach to address a specific issue or condition.

Main Points

Most Individualized Support Plans (ISPs), or treatment plans, will look similar from agency or organization to organization. The reason for this is that the AMHI consent decree requires that the ISP have specific parts and that specific goals are addressed.

Cover Page

The cover page of an ISP should contain identifying information such as: Name, Date of ISP, Date of Birth, Social Security Number, Funding Source, Address, Telephone Number, and Class Member Status. Additionally, the provider information should also be presented on the front page, and should include: Provider Name, Contact Information, Agency, Address, Whether or not there is a service agreement and releases on file, a summary of the client's treatment, and any special accommodations needed for the client.

Individualized Treatment Plan

☐Initial ☐90-Day Review ☐ Annual			Client Information				Client #:	
Name:		Date:		DOB:		SS#:		
Funding Source:			Funding Source Policy#:			Crisis Potential:		
Current Address:				Telephone:		Cell#		
Dx:				Class Member:				
Dx2:				Guardian:				
Provider Information								
Provider:						Telephone:		
Agency/Address:								
(Check) Is there a service agreement needed? ☐ Yes ☐ No				Releases reviewed: ☐updated ☐no changes required				
Narrative								
Special Accommodations Needed								

Goal Page

In Maine, as required by the AMHI consent decree, the treatment plan must consider 14 specific areas, with some goals being specifically required, such as the mental health goal. The specific goal areas are as follows:

1. Housing

2. Financial

3. Education

4. Social/Recreation/Peer Support

    A. Family

    B. Culture/Gender

    C. Recreation/Social

    D. Peer Support

5. Transportation

6. Health Care

    A. Dental

    B. Eye Care

    C. Hearing Health

    D. Medical

7. Vocational

8. Legal

9. Living Skills

10. Substance Abuse

11. Mental Health

    A. Trauma

    B. Emotional/Psychological

    C. Psychiatric/Medications

    D. Crisis

12. Spiritual

13. Outreach

14. Other (specify)

Each goal is specifically assigned to its placement on the list; for example, an 11.B goal, Mental Health-Psychological, is the same numeric designation across the mental health and substance use disorder field in Maine. These goals should be listed on a separate page, and each one should be addressed. It must be documented that each goal was assessed, otherwise, if an audit occurs, there will be citations (again, it is legally required under the AMHI consent decree).

Planning Page

On the third page of the ISP, the client's name should be included, along with a client number or account number. The presenting problem should be documented in its own section. The long-term goal should be noted in its own section also. For example, the Long Term Goal would be one of the goals from the goal page. Additionally, the target date should be noted and is usually for one year.

The following section should be broken down into four areas: Short Term Goal, Client Objectives (steps on how the short-term goal will be met; should include methods, frequency, and should be measurable), Who is responsible (family, friends, staff, other providers), and a section for when the goals were met, and room for comments. Lastly, the plan must include strengths and weaknesses. Whenever possible, use the client's own words. A planning page might look like the following:

Name:	John Fictitious	Client #:	1234			

Presenting Problem:
"I have difficulty making my counseling appointments."

Long Term Goal # (target date is 1 year): 11.B Mental Health-Psychological			Target Date: 1/22/2025

Short Term Goal (Include Goal # and Target Date within 6 months)	CLIENT OBJECTIVES (Methods/Frequency) AND Action Steps (measurable)	Who is Responsible? (family, friends, staff, other providers, etc)	Date Met/Comments
"My counseling sessions sometimes sneak up on me, then I get anxious and cancel"	1. I will meet with my case manager every 90 days. 2. I will discuss how I am feeling. 3. We will go over my schedule at least once a week. 4. I will make time for my counseling appointments. 5. I will use the Lyft app. to schedule rides.	Me Case Manager	4/22/24 Client is meeting 1, 2, 3, and has attended 5 of 6 appointments

Strengths (Personal & Resource):
"I have a strong will to succeed."

Barriers (Personal & Resource):
"I don't have transportation."

In many cases, and cases of homelessness, providers may note a need for 1. Housing. For 2. Financial, the State will not authorize payment, because they believe that representative payees are assigned by the government, such as a Social Security Representative Payee, a Trustee (probate court), a Conservator (probate court), etc., which has its funding mechanism.

Most of the goals are self-explanatory, up to 5. Transportation. Working to establish transportation for the client, such as MaineCare-funded bus rides, or coordination with MaineCare-funded and licensed agencies, may be billable; however, billing for providing rides is not a mental health or addiction reimbursable service.

If the service being provided is a mental health billable service, then the ISP must contain an 11.B Emotional/Psychological goal. Agencies who provide services, and bill under mental health, will not be approved by utilization reviews, to bill for mental health services, without noting the goal. This is the same for substance abuse; if billing for substance abuse, there must be a 10. Substance Abuse goal.

It has been my experience that utilization reviews, do not usually approve 13. Outreach goals because they are ambiguous. They are the 'catch-all' for any service that might have been provided outside of the treatment plan, though necessary, but undocumented. I recommend including a 13. Outreach goal, so that if there are issues that need to be addressed outside of the treatment plan, they may still be covered for billing.

Treatment plans may include numerous goals; however, particular care must be made to ensure that clients are not overwhelmed by them. In my experience, three goals are manageable. I usually select goals such as 1. Housing (if needed), 11.B Emotional/Psychiatric, and 13. Outreach.

Signature Page

On the signature page, the Criteria for Discharge are required to be discussed. In my experience, the criteria can be as simple as "Client will be discharged when he has been incident-free for one year and is in full remission."

If there are unmet needs, those should be noted on the signature page also. There must be a section for it, and there must be documentation that it was considered; otherwise, a citation may be issued. In most instances, it is okay to note, "None". Generally, an unmet need occurs when it has been at least a year since the goal was noted on the ISP and unmet. In most cases, those goals can be renewed for the follow-on year. However, if there is a real unmet need, the Consent Decree Coordinator (often referred to as the 'CDC', at the Maine DHHS, Office of Behavioral Health), should be notified, and collaborated with to look for solutions. If the provider fails to notify the CDC, and the unmet need is uncovered during audits or entered into the utilization review system, the Court Master may be notified, which will result in DHHS officials being berated. So...they are more than happy to help when unmet needs are identified.

In the meeting notes, it is important to note that all 14 goals were reviewed, as well as vocation and employment, so that state officials responsible for auditing know that required goal areas and concerns are being addressed.

The ISP must be reviewed every 90 days and updated with the assessment annually. Both documents should be updated as needed. There should always be an option for the client to make comments. It is also a good practice to note, in the treatment record, if the client declined or requested a copy of the treatment plan.

One of the most frequent citations I have seen over the years, on ISPs, is the failure of providers to list their relative credentials, after their signatures. In the mental health and substance use disorder field, it is a requirement on treatment records for providers to also note their credentials after their name and signature.

Lastly, the clinical supervisor should review the assessment, and the ISP, within 30 days of its completion.

Name:		Client #:		
Criteria for Discharge:				
Unmet Service Needs:				
Meeting Notes:				
All 14 goals and vocational/employment were discussed.				
This Plan Review Due by (date):		**Next Plan Review Due :**		
If Review Completed After Due Date, Reason:				
Comments of Person Receiving Services:	No Comment, Please Check ☐ , and Initial .			
I declare that I have participated in (Agency Name Here) intake process and the development of this treatment plan. I have been advised of both the risks and benefits of these services. ___ I do or ___ do not want a copy of this plan.				
Copy of Plan Sent to Client/Guardian on (Date):		**By Whom:**		
Signature of Person Receiving Services:			**Date:**	
Signature of Guardian (if applicable):			**Date:**	
Signature of Clinical Supervisor:			**Date:**	
The goals and objectives of this plan correlate with those identified as Daily Living Support Service needs according to client's ISP.				
Signature of Case Manager:			**Date:**	
Sent copy of plan to Case Manager on (date):				

Conclusion

While most treatment plans appear similar across agencies, this results from a mandate rather than a lack of individualization. The AMHI consent decree dictates specific components and goals for Individualized Support Plans. However, creating a valid and audit-proof treatment plan requires a thorough assessment as its foundation. Without this assessment, the plan holds no credibility, and agencies risk citations during audits. In essence, while the framework might be shared, the content of each ISP should be carefully tailored to the specific needs and goals identified through a rigorous assessment process.

6. Crisis Plan

Introduction

The goal of mental health crisis planning is to prevent and get ready for the worst-case situation for a client's mental health. This could involve their symptoms getting worse to the point where they endanger themselves or others.

Encouraging clients to take charge of their care, by empowering them to recognize their triggers, and responses, and to feel like they're part of their treatment, is one of the main objectives of this kind of planning. The crisis plan provides a map for the client, and the provider when the client is struggling. Providers often recommend the client keep their crisis plan, somewhere nearby, to refer to if needed.

Main Points

I have always hated the term 'crisis plan' because it implies that eventually, the client is going to go into crisis. Likewise, if a client has never had a crisis plan, and does not need one, then I do not usually do one. If this is the case, then it should be documented in the summary on the ISP, that a crisis plan is not needed at this time. Generally, I have always referred to the crisis plan as a wellness plan, and presented it to clients that way: "What do you feel we need to do to keep you well?", "What signs indicate you are not doing well?", etc.

Triggers can be as simple as, "Noise", "Aggression", "Yelling at me", "Talking to me when I don't want to talk", etc. Likewise, in the 'What is not helpful section?', I have seen, "Calling the police", "Continuing to talk to me", etc. Some of the most popular comments I have seen, for what is helpful, was, "Listen to music", "Go for a walk", "Talk with my counselor", etc.

Probably the most important part of the form is who to involve. It is important to have accurate numbers, that have been verified. There should be a release on file for each of the individuals if they are not agency staff. The remaining sections of the form are fairly obvious; and again, providers need to include their credentials when writing their name or signing their name on the form.

Keep the document simple and easy to refer to.

Wellness Plan

Client Name:	Treatment Plan Date:
Triggers and Progression:	What actions are helpful?
What is not helpful?	

Who to involve?

Name _____ Relationship _____ Phone _____

Name _____ Relationship _____ Phone _____

Name _____ Relationship _____ Phone _____

Prior Risk to Self or Others:
Additional Notes:

Client signature: _____ Date: _____

Case manager signature: _____ Date: _____

Conclusion

Rather than solely preparing for "crisis," this approach renames mental health planning as a "wellness plan" to empower clients in managing their well-being. Instead of assuming a crisis will happen, it focuses on identifying individual triggers and helpful coping mechanisms. The plan, easily accessible to the client and provider, includes support contacts and clear steps for both proactive wellness and navigating challenging situations. This shift prioritizes prevention and ownership, potentially reducing the need for "crisis" intervention altogether.

7. Progress Note

Introduction

The purpose of the progress note in mental health treatment is to document client-centered details about the length, type, content, and interventions of a case management meeting or therapy session. Progress notes are then used by other providers to review the client's treatment history and progress toward therapeutic goals and are often viewed by third parties such as insurance companies.

The goal of progress notes is to provide a comprehensive, clear, and accurate representation of the client's therapeutic journey. They act as a common thread that links all healthcare providers involved in the client's care, ensuring continuity of treatment, and facilitating collaboration between teams.

In addition to recording relevant objective data such as test results, documents, and other medical information, the progress note also includes subjective data such as a client's direct quotes, experiences, feelings, thoughts, etc. It also lists the specific treatment techniques applied throughout the appointment and the broader field they fall into, for example, cognitive restructuring within CBT or relaxation techniques as part of mindfulness training.

The final step in the progress note is to record a plan for the client's next steps between sessions, including any changes to the original treatment plans set out at the intake or time of assessment and treatment planning. This may also include the identification of new goals, a different approach to an existing problem, or simply an agreed-upon next step in the client's path toward recovery.

Main Points

The enclosed progress note is a brief draft I created based on the rules, regulations, and my experiences as a provider.

The demographic information is fairly self-explanatory. The provider should add their credentials at the top, and by their signature at the bottom. The reason I do this is so that I have an increased chance that the provider will place their credentials (again, this is a legal requirement).

The duration times should match that of the Units. On occasion, providers will bill for initial contact (the first contact of the day less than 15 minutes), which may be allowable by MaineCare and other insurance policies. I like to include subsequent times on the note, because, especially during a crisis, there may be a need to keep a running note.

The provider must note the kind of contact on the note, for example, face to face (note, 'FF'), telephone (note, 'Cell'), video conferences such as Zoom (note, 'Zoom'), collateral, or contact with other providers or family (note, 'C'), etc. It is very difficult to convince officials that billing should be allowable for text messages. If billing for text messages, a copy of those messages should be included with the notes (note, 'Text').

Documenting whether the client is in crisis, or a potential need, helps determine the urgency of the service, intensity of the service, and need for follow-up services. It also helps document when the client is not in crisis. Oftentimes, a crisis is a critical reportable event, to the Office of Behavioral Health, and a note will likely be requested during an official review of the report.

The provider must be sure that the service provided is tied to a goal or goals, and discuss how it is related. Clinical auditors are looking for the 'Golden Thread'; how services are tied together. Likewise, the narrative must be clear and discuss how the services contribute to the client's treatment and wellness journey.

Progress Note

Name:_____   Date:_____

DOB:_____

Clinician:_____ Credentials:_____ Contact Type:_____

Duration in Units (1 unit=15 minutes):_____   Time:_____ to:_____
Subsequent Time:_____ to: _____; Time:_____ to:_____; Time:_____ to:_____

Services Provided: __Case Management __Counseling __Addiction Counseling __Other
Goal Areas (tied to treatment plan):

Is this note documenting a crisis?__Yes __No
Is there a potential need for crisis intervention or resolution?__Yes __No

Narrative

Comments on progress toward goals:

Provider Signature_____ Credentials_____ Date_____

Clinical Supervisor Review: __Yes __No Initials:_____

Conclusion

In mental health, progress notes act as detailed records of each session, capturing key details like duration, content, interventions, and client responses. These notes, accessible to healthcare providers and sometimes third parties, offer a comprehensive picture of the client's journey, enabling collaboration, informed interventions, and tailored treatment plans. They balance objective data (e.g., assessment results) with subjective experiences (client quotes, emotions), and outline the next steps towards recovery, ensuring continuity and a unified approach to the client's well-being.

8. Discharge Planning

Introduction

Discharge planning is part of treatment planning. Discharge planning is a crucial process for ensuring a smooth and successful transition from one service to follow-on care, or back to the community. It should focus on preparing the individual for independent living and continued support for their mental health needs. Once the client is discharged from care, there will need to be follow-up. If the individual is a class member, then the agency will need the permission of the CDC to discharge the client. Permission can be gained by contacting the Office of Behavioral Health.

Main Points

The discharge plan should be noted on the treatment plan. The discharge summary is part of the client record. A follow-up, after the discharge, should also be part of the plan.

The demographic portion of the discharge summary should include whether the individual is a class member. These clients have special considerations, under Maine law, and may require the involvement of the state, before discharging. The form should also include the reason for discharge and the diagnosis.

Goals and progress should be discussed on the discharge summary, for follow on providers, as well as housing status, vocation, etc. Special attention should be given to medications, to ensure the client has access after discharge; this is especially important if the client is prescribed medication by the provider.

The Likert scale for SUD discharges is designed, per the rules and regulations, to provide evidence of progress, or lack of progress, in treatment. The scale can be used for both mental health and substance use disorder services.

If the client is being discharged because they have become an inactive client, for some unknown reason, it is best to send a 30-day letter. The 30-day letter simply states that the client's service will be terminated after 30 days, due to inactivity, or other reasons, unless the client gets in touch with the provider. Again, the provider may need to request permission to discharge the client if they are a class member.

Lastly, and as discussed previously, providers, who are completing the discharge paperwork, must sign the form and provide their credentials.

DISCHARGE SUMMARY

Consumer Name:_____   Client ID#:_____
Services Provided: __Case Management __Counseling __Addiction Counseling
Date of Admission:_____ Date of Discharge:_____ Class Member: __Yes __No

Reason for Discharge:_____
Diagnosis:

Assessment of Services

Goals	Progress
1.	1.
2.	2.
3.	3.
4.	4.

Likert Scales below required for SUD discharges		
Overall Physical/Medical Health and Mental Health Status At Time of Intake		
Client perception of physical/medical health:		☐ 1 ☐ 2 ☐ 3 ☐ 4 ☐ 5 ☐ 6 ☐ 7 ☐ 8 ☐ 9 ☐ 10
Client perception of mental health:		☐ 1 ☐ 2 ☐ 3 ☐ 4 ☐ 5 ☐ 6 ☐ 7 ☐ 8 ☐ 9 ☐ 10
Provider perception of physical/medical health:		☐ 1 ☐ 2 ☐ 3 ☐ 4 ☐ 5 ☐ 6 ☐ 7 ☐ 8 ☐ 9 ☐ 10
Provider perception of mental health:		☐ 1 ☐ 2 ☐ 3 ☐ 4 ☐ 5 ☐ 6 ☐ 7 ☐ 8 ☐ 9 ☐ 10
Overall Physical/Medical Health and Mental Health Status At Time of Discharge		
Client perception of physical/medical health:		☐ 1 ☐ 2 ☐ 3 ☐ 4 ☐ 5 ☐ 6 ☐ 7 ☐ 8 ☐ 9 ☐ 10
Client perception of mental health:		☐ 1 ☐ 2 ☐ 3 ☐ 4 ☐ 5 ☐ 6 ☐ 7 ☐ 8 ☐ 9 ☐ 10
Provider perception of physical/medical health:		☐ 1 ☐ 2 ☐ 3 ☐ 4 ☐ 5 ☐ 6 ☐ 7 ☐ 8 ☐ 9 ☐ 10
Provider perception of mental health:		☐ 1 ☐ 2 ☐ 3 ☐ 4 ☐ 5 ☐ 6 ☐ 7 ☐ 8 ☐ 9 ☐ 10
Note: Please rate with 1 being very poor and 10 being very good		

Employment upon discharge:

Housing upon discharge:

Summary of Treatment:

Strengths and needs:

Crisis Interventions:

Recommendations:

Need for referral for continued service:

Need for medication:

30-day letter: __Yes __No, If no, reason: _____

Provider Signature:_____Credentials:_____Date:_____
Print Name:_____

Supervisor Signature:_____Credentials:_____Date:_____
Print Name:_____

Conclusion

To ensure a smooth transition from mental health and substance use disorder care, discharge planning starts within the treatment plan itself. It focuses on client independence, continued support, and follow-up care. Class members may need state involvement before discharge.

Appendix A: Client Record

1. Referral form

Agency Letterhead

Referral type: __Peer Support ___Case Management ___Counseling ___SA Counseling

Client Name: Date of Birth: SS#

Class Member:

Insurance & Policy Number:

Physical Address:

Mailing Address:

Diagnosis: Diagnosed by:

Guardian Name: Guardian Phone:

Interpreter needed:

Home phone:

Permission to leave a message?

Referral Source Name/Organization:

Referral Source Address:

Referral Source Contact Phone: Fax:

Referral Source Email Address:

Reason for Referral:

Dangerous variables (please include recent crisis/hospitalizations, incarcerations, violent or aggressive behavior, contagious medical conditions, criminal history, risk to self or others, or other pertinent safety information):

Mental Health Providers:

Other Information:

Signature of the person making the referral: Date:

For office use only:

Date Referral Received: Time Received:

Insurance Verification Information: Date Verified:

Verified By:

Note: Include agency information in the footer, so that providers know where to send the fax. It's best to post referral forms on the agency website in a conspicuous area.

2. Intake Checklist

Client Name: Date of Intake:

Class Member:

Required Intake Forms:

__AC/OK

__State Utilization Review Approval

(normally completed after the intake)

__Comprehensive Assessment

__Demographics Form (Face Sheet)

__Intake Progress Note

__Individualized Treatment Plan (ISP)

__LOCUS

__Referral

__Rights of Recipients Summary

__Welcome Packet (Privacy Notice, Confidentiality, etc.)

__Wellness Plan

Required Releases:

__Crisis Agency

(CHCS, Crisis & Counseling, Spring Harbor, Mid-Coast Mental Health,

Sweetser, Tri-County Mental Health, Evergreen, or Oxford County Mental

Health; depends on the region of the client)

__DHHS

__Emergency Contact

__HealthInfoNet (if needed)

__Housing

__Primary Care Physician (PCP)

__Psychiatrist

__Therapist

__Social Security (if needed)

Outside Information:

Diagnosis: Provider of Dx: Date:

Guardianship Papers Needed:

Other Records Requests:

3. Welcome Packet

To document that the welcome packet was received, create a form for the client to sign. Many of the required forms can be located online. The record must document the following was received:

- Welcome Packet

- Service Agreement

- Client Statement of Understanding for Payment of Services

- Consent to Treat

- Fee Schedule

- Notice of Privacy Practices

- Substance Abuse Records and Confidentiality Statement

- Smoking Education and Referral Information

4. Rights of Recipients

Universal Summary of the *Rights of Recipients of Mental Health Services*-Community Based Outpatient

This is a summary of your rights as a recipient of community-based services under the *Rights of Recipients of Mental Health Services* and the *Rights of Recipients of Mental Health Services Who Are Children In Need of Treatment.*

You have a right to obtain a full copy of these rights from the agency currently serving you or from the Maine Department of Health and Human Services, Office of Substance Abuse and Mental Health Services (SAMHS), 11 State House Station-Marquardt Building, second floor, Augusta, Maine 04333, Tel # (207) 287-4243, TTY #: 1-800-606-0215 or the Office of Children's Behavioral Health Services (OCFS), 2 Anthony Avenue, Augusta, Maine 04333, Tel # (207) 287-4251, TTY #: 1-800-606-0215. If you are deaf or do not understand English, an interpreter will be made available to you so that you can understand your rights.

1. Basic Rights: You have the same civil, human, and legal rights which all citizens have. You have a right to be treated with courtesy and full respect for you individuality and dignity at all times.

2. Confidentiality and Access to Records: You have the right to have your records kept confidential and only released with your fully informed and signed consent. If a guardian has been authorized to make decisions for you, the guardian has the right to release records. You have the right to review your record at any reasonable time. You may add written comments to your record to clarify information you believe is inaccurate or incomplete. No one else can see your record unless you specifically authorize them to see it, except in instances described in the *Rights of Recipients of Mental Health Services.*

3. Individualized Treatment Plan: You have the right to an individualized treatment plan, developed by you and your worker or treatment team, based upon your needs and goals. The plan must be in writing. You have the right to a copy of your plan. The plan must specifically detail what everyone involved in your treatment will do, the time frames in which the tasks and goals will be accomplished and how success will be determined. The plan must be based upon your actual needs and goals. If a needed service is not available, the plan must detail how that need will be met.

4. Informed Consent: No services or treatment can be provided to you against your will. If you have a guardian, he or she is authorized to make decisions without your consent. You have the right to be informed of the possible risks and anticipated benefits of all treatment, including medications, in a manner which you understand. If you have any questions, you may ask your worker or anyone else you choose before making decisions about treatment or services. If a

guardian has been authorized to make decisions for you, the guardian has the right to be fully informed of all risks and benefits or proposed treatment.

5. Assistance in the Protection of Rights: You have the right to appoint a representative of your choice to help you understand your rights, protect your rights or help you work out a treatment plan. If you wish to have a representative, you must designate this person in writing. You can have access to the representative at any time and you can change or cancel the designation at any time.

6. Freedom from Seclusion and Restraint: You cannot be secluded or restrained in the community setting.

7. Right to File a Grievance: You have the right to bring a grievance to challenge any violation of your rights or any questionable practices. You have the right to have your grievance answered in writing, with reasons for the decisions. You may appeal any decision to the Office of Children's Behavioral Health Services. You may not be punished in any way for filing a grievance. You cannot be retaliated against for filing a grievance. For more information about your rights or for help with filing a grievance, contact:

For more information about your rights or for help with filing a grievance, contact:

Grievance Coordinator	Disability Rights Center of Maine
11 SHS, Marquardt Bldg. 2nd Floor	PO Box 2007,
Augusta, Maine 04333	Augusta Maine 04338
Tel # 287-4249	Tel # 1-800-452-1948.

_____

| Date | Client Signature | Date | Witness Signature |

_____

| Date | Guardian Signature | Date | Witness Signature |

_____

Date   Employee Signature (New Hires Only)

5. Demographics (Face Sheet)

Demographics and Identifying Information

Demographics		
Client Name:	Date of Birth:	Class Member:
Address: City: State:	Zip Code:	
Home Phone: Cell phone:	Okay to leave a message? __Y __N	
Gender __M __F Marital Status: __Partnered __Married __Single __Other		
SS #:		
Guardian Name: Relationship to Client:		
Guardian Phone: Guardian Address:		
Closest Relative Name, Relationship, Address and Phone:		
Client Occupation and/or Source of Income:		
Clients Medications (Current):		
Clients Allergies/Drug Interactions:		
Are you currently receiving mental health outpatient therapy or substance abuse services from another provider? __Y __N If yes, provider name/agency:		
MaineCare		
Name: Client MaineCare Number: Expiration:		
Other Insurance Carrier		
Insurance Provider: Guarantor:		
Guarantor Employer: Guarantor SS#:		
Policy Number: Group #:		
Insurance Provider Address: Guarantor DOB:		
City: State/Zip: Telephone #:		
Co-Pay: Referral Needed __Y __N Referral #:		
Primary Care Physician: Telephone #:		

Billing Policy/Consent for Treatment

I understand that I am financially responsible to (Agency Name Here) for services not covered by my insurance unless I am also covered under MaineCare. I also understand that I am personally responsible for missed appointments if I have not notified (Agency Name Here) 24 hours in advance.

I hereby authorize (Agency Name Here) to furnish information regarding my diagnosis and treatment to the above insurance carriers and/or MaineCare.

I hereby authorize permission for treatment by providers of (Agency Name Here).

Client/Guardian Signature:_____Date:_____

6. Diagnosis or Diagnosis Verification Form

Section 17 Clinical Eligibility Opinion/Verification Form

Date:

Client: Date of Birth:

Social Security Number:

Service Requested: __Peer Support __Case Management __Counseling __SA Counseling

Class Member:

The above member meets the eligibility criteria as set forth in the current published version of Maine Care Benefits, based on documented or reported history, where he/she is likely to have future episodes, related to mental illness, with a non-excluded DSM-5 diagnosis, that would result in or have significant risk factors of homelessness, criminal justice involvement or require a mental health inclient treatment greater than 72 hours, or residential treatment unless community support program services are provided; based on documented or reported history. My opinion is that the member has a strong likelihood of becoming:

__Homeless __Hospitalized __Involved w/Criminal Justice System __Placed in Residential Treatment

My opinion is based off of the following (Check all those that apply):

__Documented History __Reported History __As the treating clinician/doctor

__LOCUS Score is: _____

The reported history was obtained from:

__Oral history from the client   __Oral history from a provider

__Written history from the member   __Written history from a provider

Brief Explanation:

Doctor/Clinician Signature:

Doctor/Clinician Print Name and Credentials:

7. Level of Care Utilization System (LOCUS) (In Maine, we use the LOCUS, instead of ASAM criteria).

To learn more about LOCUS, visit:

https://www.maine.gov/dhhs/sites/maine.gov.dhhs/files/documents/obh/mentalhealth/mh-system/Webinars/LOCUS-ANSA-Powerpoint.pdf

ADULT LOCUS SCORING SHEET
Adult Level of Care Determination

Name: _____   Screening Date [_____]

Service Start Date _____

Case # _____ MaineCare # _____   DOB _____ Gender _____

Rater Scorer Name _____   Rater Scorer ID [_____]

Consumer's County of Residence _____ Region ☐ I ☐ II ☐ III

Agency Program Name: Maine Behavioral Health Organization

Check Service Type ☐ CIS ☐ Grant ☐ BHH ☐ DLS

Locus Administration: ☐ Baseline or entry ☐ Update ☐ Annual ☐ Exit from services

1. Calculation of Locus Composite Score						
Dimension	Dimension Ratings					Rating
I. Risk of Harm	1	2	3	4*	5	
II. Functional Status	1	2	3	4*	5	
III. Medical, Addictive and Psychiatric Co-Morbidity	1	2	3	4*	5	
IV. Recovery Environment						
A. Level of Stress	1	2	3	4	5	
B. Level of Support	1	2	3	4	5	
V. Treatment and Recovery	1	2	3	4	5	
VI. Attitude and Engagement	1	2	3	4	5	
Composite LOCUS Score (Add numbers in right column)						
2. LOCUS - Derived Level of Care Recommendation (consult Determination Grid)						
3. Actual (Disposition) Level of Care						
4. Reasons for deviation from LOCUS - derived level of care recommendation:						
(Must be completed if the actual LOC disposition (#3) is different from the Locus - derived LOC (#2)						

Note: Bolded Dimension Ratings indicate Independent Criteria (IC). When IC is met, Admission to the designated level is required regardless of the Composite Score.

Level of Safety: Assign to Level V if scale score is 4; Assign to Level VI if scale score is 5.

*Level of Functioning and C0-Occurring Conditions (Co-Morbidity): Assign to Level V if scale is a 4 and the sum of IVA (Level of Stress) and IVB (Level of Support) is greater that 2; Assign to Level VI if scale score is 5.

Exception: If the functional Status and/or the Co-Occurring Score is 4 and the sum of IVA and IVB is 2, the Composite Score determines level of care.

	Level of Care	Recovery Maintenance Health Maintenance	Low Intensity Community Based Services	High Intensity Community Based Services	Medically Monitored Non-Residential Services	Medically Monitored Residential Services	Medically Managed Residential Services
Dimensions		Level 1	Level 2	Level 3	Level 4	Level 5	Level 6
I	Risk of Harm	2 or less	2 or less	3 or less	3 or less	④ 5	⑤ 6
II	Functional Status	2 or less	2 or less	3 or less	3 or less	④+ 5	⑤ 6
III	Co-Morbidity	2 or less	2 or less	3 or less	3 or less	④+ 5	⑤ 6
IV A	Recovery Environment "Stress"	Sum of IV A + IV B is 4 or less	Sum of IV A + IV B is 5 or less	Sum of IV A + IV B is 5 or less	3 or 4	4 or more	4 or more
IV B	Recovery Environment "Support"				3 or less	4 or more	4 or more
V	Treatment & Recovery History	2 or less	2 or less	3 or less	3 or 4	3 or more	4 or more
VI	Engagement	2 or less	2 or less	3 or less	3 or 4	3 or more	4 or more
	Composite Rating	10 to 13	14 to 16	17 to 19	20 to 22	23 to 27	28 or more

Rater Signature & Credentials _____   Date _____

8. AC/OK

There are screenings for both adults and children. To read more about this screening, please visit: https://ccsme.org/wp-content/uploads/2017/02/AC-OK-Screening-tool.pdf.

AC-OK: ADULT Screen for Co-Occurring Disorders
(Mental Health, Trauma-Related Mental Health Issues & Substance Abuse)

First Name: _____ Last Name: _____

Gender: _____ Date of Birth: _____ Date of Screening: _____

During the past year:

1. Have you experienced serious depression (felt sadness, hopelessness, loss of interest, change of appetite or sleep pattern, difficulty going about your daily activities)? ☐ Yes ☐ No

2. Have you experienced thoughts of harming yourself? ☐ Yes ☐ No

3. Have you experienced a period when your thinking speeds up and you have trouble keeping up with your thoughts? ☐ Yes ☐ No

4. Have you attempted suicide? ☐ Yes ☐ No

5. Have you had periods where you felt that you could not trust family or friends? ☐ Yes ☐ No

6. Have you been prescribed medication for any psychological or emotional problems? ☐ Yes ☐ No

7. Have you experienced hallucinations (heard or seen things others do not hear or see)? ☐ Yes ☐ No
   Mental Health   Questions 1-7 Total yes answers: _____

8. Have you ever been hit, slapped, kicked, emotionally or sexually hurt, or threatened by someone? ☐ Yes ☐ No

9. Have you experienced a traumatic event and since had repeated nightmares/dreams and/or anxiety that interferes with you leading a normal life? ☐ Yes ☐ No
   Trauma   Questions 8-9 Total yes answers: _____

10. Have you been preoccupied with drinking alcohol and/or using other drugs? ☐ Yes ☐ No

11. Have you experienced problems caused by drinking alcohol and/or using other drugs, and you kept using? ☐ Yes ☐ No

12. Do you, at times, drink alcohol and/or use other drugs more than you intended? ☐ Yes ☐ No

13. Have you needed to drink more alcohol and/or use more drugs to get the same effect you used to get with less? ☐ Yes ☐ No

14. Do you, at times, drink alcohol and/or use other drugs to alter the way you feel? ☐ Yes ☐ No

15. Have you tried to stop drinking alcohol and/or using other drugs, but couldn't? ☐ Yes ☐ No
    Substance Abuse   Questions 10-15 Total yes answers: _____

Provider Representative Signature: _____

Comprehensive Assessment

Demographics

Name: Date:

Physical Address:

Phone Number:

Date of Birth:

Age:

Social Security Number:

Gender:

Military Status:

Guardian:

      Guardian Name:

      Guardian Address:

      Guardian Phone Number:

Emergency Contact:

      Emergency Contact Name:

      Emergency Contact Address:

      Emergency Contact Phone Number:

Class Member:

Mental Health Advance Directive on File:

      If not, the reason:

Was a Mental Health Advance Directive Offered:

Was there a crisis intervention in the last year?

      Is there a potential for crisis in the future?

Is there a crisis or wellness plan on file?

Service Need & Support

Orientation: __Person __Place __Time __Situation __Disoriented

Speech: __WNL __Low __Loud __Mumbled __Slurred __Rapid __Pressured

Eye Contact: __WNL __Avoiding __Staring __Tracking __Wandering __Fleeting

Appearance: __Clean/Groomed __Disheveled __Unkempt __Severe Deficit

Describe Appearance:

Motor Activity: __WNL __Lethargic __Psychomotor Agitation

__Psychomotor Retardation __Tics __Tardive Dyskinesia __Altered Gait __Falls:

Describe Motor Activity:

Energy Level: __WNL __Increased __Decreased __Variable __Vegetive

Sleep: __WNL __Increased __Decreased __Variable __Interrupted

Appetite: __WNL __Increased __Decreased __Variable

Libido: __ Not Evaluated __WNL __Increased __Decreased __Variable __No Interest

Memory: __WNL __Impaired

Concentration: __WNL __Increased __Decreased __Easily Distracted

Cognition: __WNL __Mild __Moderate __Severe

Potential dangerous variables:

History supporting a request for services:

Strengths and weaknesses relative to treatment:

Leisure, social, or recreational interests:

Family and support system's perception of needs for services:

Previous history of outclient services:

Previous psychiatric hospitalization (starting with most recent; include dates):

Previous medical hospitalization:

Crisis intervention:

History of suicidal or homicidal behavior:

Family history of mental illness or suicide:

Diagnosis

Mental Health Diagnosis:

    Diagnosis codes and descriptions:

    Therapist: Date:

    Agency:

    Other (LOCUS, CANS, ANSA)

    Name: Rater ID: Date:

If a therapist has not been identified, is one needed?

If one has been identified, who?

    Agency:

How long have these services been provided?

Is there a psychiatrist involved?

If one has been identified, who?

Agency:

How long have these services been provided?

Current Mental Health Status

__Mood: __WNL __Sad/Depressed __Angry Irritable __Manic __Hypomanic __N/A

Other assessments of mood:

__Affect: __Full Range __Restricted __Flat __Labile __Tearful __Blunted __N/A

Is the affect congruent with mood?

Behavioral presentation: __Cooperative __Uncooperative __Engaging

__Withdrawn __Passive __Threatening__ Domineering __N/A

Other assessments of affect:

__Through Process: __WNL __Confused __Flight of Ideas __Distracted __

__Perseveration __Loose Associations __Circumstantial __Tangential

__Rumination __Other:

__Thought Interference: __None __Thought Insertion __Persecutory __Obsessive

__Compulsive __Other:

__Hallucinations: __None __Visual __Auditory __Tactile __Olfactory __Gustatory

__Command

Describe Hallucinations:

__Delusions: __None __Bizarre __Non-Bizarre __Paranoid __Religious __Persecutory

__Grandiose

Describe Delusions:

__**Orientated** (refer to Service Need & Support section): __Yes __No

Trauma & Abuse

__Abuse: __None __Sexual __Emotional __Neglect __Rape

    Was abuse ever reported? __Yes __No

    If 'Yes', to whom, and when?

    Additional information:

__Domestic Violence: __None __Past __Present

    If present, is help desired?

    Perpetrator of domestic violence:

    Describe domestic violence:

    Flashbacks:

    Additional Information:

Substance Use and Abuse

History of substance use and abuse:

Past substance use disorder treatment (when, where, program):

Current substance use (type, duration, pattern, frequency, other pertinent information):

Seeking treatment for substance use disorders: __Yes __No __Undecided

    If yes, from what:

Stages of Change: __Relapse __Pre-contemplation __Contemplation __Determination

__Action __Maintenance

If sober, how long?

What are risk factors for relapse?

Medical Conditions & History

Primary Care Physician: __Yes __No Doctor's Name:

Practice:

Other current medical providers:

Current Medical Conditions:

Past Medical Conditions:

Allergies: __No __Yes

If yes, list:

Has a neurological assessment ever been completed?

Is there a history of brain injury? __No __Yes

If yes, when, how, and was there any previous treatment?

Nutritional Assessment? __Needed __Requested __N/A

Family history of medical issues:

Dentist: __Yes __No Doctor's Name:

Practice:

Current Dental Assessment and Conditions: __N/A __Assessment Needed

Medications

Medication Name	Prescriber	Frequency	Dose

Past Medication Taken:

Medication Name	Prescriber	Frequency	Dose

Other pertinent medical information:

Familial History & Childhood Development

Birthplace:

Parent's Marital Status: __N/A __Married __Divorced __Separated

Father's Name:

      If alive, where does he reside?

Relationship dynamics:

If deceased, when and cause?

Mother's Name:

      If alive, where does she reside?

Relationship dynamics:

If deceased, when and cause?

Siblings (List in birth order):

Describe relationships with siblings:

Assessment of developmental milestones:

Describe significant childhood events:

Additional sources of support:

Social History

Marital Status:

Marital History:

Personal relationships assessment:

Children and ages:

If children are underage, where do they reside?

Spiritual/Religion

Religious Preference:

Spiritual Beliefs:

Environment/Housing/Financial

Rent Subsidy: __Yes __No If 'Yes', What kind?

Section 8: __Yes __No If pending, date of application:

Sources of Income: __SSDI __SSI/Survivor __SSI/SSDI __TANF __General Assistance

__Other:

Pending Social Security case: __Yes __No __N/A

If Yes, date applied for?

Lawyer?

Transportation Used: __MaineCare funded __Public __Own __Other __N/A

Driver's License: __Yes __No

State ID Card: __Yes __No __Needed?

Summary/Narrative

Person completing assessment:

Credentials:

Signature:

Date:

Clinician:

Credentials:

Signature:

Date:

10. Treatment Plan

ISP Page 1

Individualized Treatment Plan

☐ Initial ☐ 90-Day Review ☐ Annual	Client Information		Client #:

Name:		Date:		DOB:		SS#:	
Funding Source:			**Funding Source Policy#:**			**Crisis Potential:**	
Current Address:			**Telephone:**			**Cell#**	
Dx:			**Class Member:**				
Dx2:			**Guardian:**				

Provider Information

Provider:			**Telephone:**	
Agency/Address:				

(Check) Is there a service agreement needed? ☐ Yes ☐ No	Releases reviewed: ☐ updated ☐ no changes required

Narrative

Special Accommodations Needed

ISP Page 2

Person receiving services:

All of the following goal areas considered in the context of the individual's recovery, regardless of notation, and as of the signature date of the ISP. The following key may be used: (Status: **GE**- Goal Established; **AN**- Assessed, No Need at this time; **AO**- Assessment On-Going; **CC**- Client chooses not to address at this time; **GA**- Goal Achieved; **C**- Continuing; **D**- Dissolved) (Unmet Need: Note needs that cannot be met by current resources and indicate why)

	Goal Areas	Status	Date
1.	Housing		
2.	Financial		
3.	Education		
4.	Social/Recreation/Peer Support		
	A. Family		
	B. Cultural/Gender		
	C. Recreational/Social		
	D. Peer Support		
5.	Transportation		
6.	Health Care		
	A. Dental		
	B. Eye Care		
	C. Hearing Health		
	D. Medical		
7.	Vocational		
8.	Legal		
9.	Living Skills		
10.	Substance Abuse		
11.	Mental Health		
	A. Trauma		
	B. Emotional/Psychological		
	C. Psychiatric/ Medications		
	D. Crisis		
12.	Spiritual		
13.	Outreach		
14.	Other (specify)		

Case Manager's signature: _____ Date: _____ Copy of ISP provided to this person receiving services on this date: _____

Supervisor's signature: _____ Date: _____ Copy of ISP forwarded to CDC on this date: _____

ISP Page 3 (Create goal pages as needed)

Name:		Client #:	

Presenting Problem:

Long Term Goal #   (target date is 1 year): | Target Date:

Short Term Goal (Include Goal # and Target Date within 6 months)	CLIENT OBJECTIVES (Methods/Frequency) AND Action Steps (measurable)	Who is Responsible? (family, friends, staff, other providers, etc)	Date Met/Comments

Strengths (Personal & Resource):

Barriers (Personal & Resource):

ISP Signature Page

Name:		Client #:	

Criteria for Discharge:

Unmet Service Needs:

Meeting Notes:

All 14 goals and vocational/employment were discussed.

This Plan Review Due by (date):		Next Plan Review Due :	

If Review Completed After Due Date, Reason:

Comments of Person Receiving Services: | No Comment, Please Check ☐ , and Initial_____ .

I declare that I have participated in (Agency Name Here) intake process and the development of this treatment plan. I have been advised of both the risks and benefits of these services. ___I do or ___do not want a copy of this plan.

Copy of Plan Sent to Client/Guardian on (Date):		By Whom:	

Signature of Person Receiving Services:	Date:
Signature of Guardian (if applicable):	Date:
Signature of Clinical Supervisor:	Date:

The goals and objectives of this plan correlate with those identified as Daily Living Support Service needs according to client's ISP.

Signature of Case Manager:	Date:
Sent copy of plan to Case Manager on (date):	

11. Crisis Plan (or Wellness Plan)

Wellness Plan

Client Name		Treatment Plan Date	

Triggers and Progression

What actions are helpful?

What is not helpful?

Who to Involve

Name		Relationship		Phone	
Name		Relationship		Phone	
Name		Relationship		Phone	

Prior Risk to self or others:

Additional Notes

Client Signature		Date	

Provider Name	

Provider Signature		Date	

12. Progress Note

Name:_____   Date:_____

DOB:_____

Clinician:_____ Credentials:_____ Contact Type: _____

Duration in Units (1 unit=15 minutes):_____   Time:_____ to:_____

Subsequent Time:_____ to: _____; Time:_____ to:_____; Time:_____ to:_____

Services Provided: __Case Management __Counseling __Addiction Counseling __Other

Goal Areas (tied to treatment plan):

Is this note documenting a crisis? __Yes __No

Is there a potential need for crisis intervention or resolution? __Yes __No

Narrative

Comments on progress toward goals:

Provider Signature_____ Credentials_____ Date_____

Clinical Supervisor Review: __Yes __No Initials:_____

DISCHARGE SUMMARY

Consumer Name:_____ Client ID#:_____

Services Provided: __Case Management __Counseling __Addiction Counseling

Date of Admission:_____ Date of Discharge:_____ Class Member: __Yes __No

Reason for Discharge:_____

Diagnosis:

Assessment of Services

Goals	Progress
1.	1.
2.	2.
3.	3.
4.	4.

Likert Scales below required for SUD discharges		
Overall Physical/Medical Health and Mental Health Status At Time of Intake		
Client perception of physical/medical health:		☐1 ☐2 ☐3 ☐4 ☐5 ☐6 ☐7 ☐8 ☐9 ☐10
Client perception of mental health:		☐1 ☐2 ☐3 ☐4 ☐5 ☐6 ☐7 ☐8 ☐9 ☐10
Provider perception of physical/medical health:		☐1 ☐2 ☐3 ☐4 ☐5 ☐6 ☐7 ☐8 ☐9 ☐10
Provider perception of mental health:		☐1 ☐2 ☐3 ☐4 ☐5 ☐6 ☐7 ☐8 ☐9 ☐10
Overall Physical/Medical Health and Mental Health Status At Time of Discharge		
Client perception of physical/medical health:		☐1 ☐2 ☐3 ☐4 ☐5 ☐6 ☐7 ☐8 ☐9 ☐10
Client perception of mental health:		☐1 ☐2 ☐3 ☐4 ☐5 ☐6 ☐7 ☐8 ☐9 ☐10
Provider perception of physical/medical health:		☐1 ☐2 ☐3 ☐4 ☐5 ☐6 ☐7 ☐8 ☐9 ☐10
Provider perception of mental health:		☐1 ☐2 ☐3 ☐4 ☐5 ☐6 ☐7 ☐8 ☐9 ☐10
Note: Please rate with 1 being very poor and 10 being very good		

Employment upon discharge:

Housing upon discharge:

Summary of Treatment:

Strengths and needs:

Crisis Interventions:

Recommendations:

Need for referral for continued service:

Need for medication:

30-day letter: __Yes __No, If no, reason: _____

Provider Signature:_____Credentials:_____Date:_____
Print Name:_____

Supervisor Signature:_____Credentials:_____Date:_____
Print Name:_____

Behavioral Health Acronyms in Maine

A

A&SQ: Ages & Stages Questionnaire

A&SQ: Ages & Stages Questionnaire (with Social-Emotional scale)

AAA: Area Agency on Aging

AAG: Assistant Attorney General

AAMHS: Alliance for Addiction and Mental Health Services

ABA: Applied Behavior Analysis

ABI: Acquired Brain Injury

ACA: Affordable Care Act

ACES: Automated Client Eligibility System

ACO: Accountable Care Organization

AC/OK: A trauma assessment

ACT: Assertive Community Treatment

ADA: Americans with Disabilities Act

ADD: Attention Deficit Disorder

ADHD: Attention Deficit Hyperactive Disorder

ADL: Activities of Daily Living

ADLs: Activities of Daily Living

AGI: Adjusted Gross Income

AIDS: Auto Immune Deficiency Disorder

AFCARS: Adoption & Foster Care Analysis Reporting System

AFFM: Adoptive and Foster Families of Maine

AG: Attorney General

ALF: Assisted Living Facility

AMHC: Aroostook Mental Health Center

ANSA: Adult Needs and Strengths Assessment

APA: American Psychiatric Association

APA: American Psychological Association

APS: Adult Protective Services

APS: Previous name of the third-party MaineCare utilization review system

ARP: Alternative Response Program

AS: Asperger's Disorder

ASI: Alternative Services Incorporated

ASD: Autism Spectrum Disorder

ASL: American Sign Language

ASM: Autism Society of Maine

ASO: Administrative Service Organization.

ASQ: Ages & Stages Questionnaire

Aspire: Additional Support for Retraining and Employment

AT: Assistive Technology

B

BCABA: Board Certified Assistant Behavior Analyst

BCBA: Board Certified Behavior Analyst

BCF: Bolduc Correctional Facility

BHH: Behavioral Health Homes (mental health under ObamaCare/ACA)

BHHO: Behavioral Health Home Organization (mental health under ObamaCare/ACA)

BHP: Behavioral Health Professional (MaineCare reimbursable in-home support)

BIIN: Brain Injury Information Network

BMHI: Bangor Mental Health Institute

BOD: Board of Directors

BRAP: Bridging Rental Assistance Program (Supplemental MaineCare program)

C

CAB: Community Advisory Board

CADC: Certified Alcohol Drug Counselor

CAFAS: Child and Adolescent Functional Assessment Scale

CANS: Child and Adolescent Needs and Strengths

CAP: Community Action Program

CARF: Commission Accreditation of Rehabilitation Facilities

CASA: Children's Advocate Support Association

CBA: Collective Bargaining Agreement

CBA: Curriculum Based Assessment

CBH: Children's Behavioral Health

CBHS: Children's Behavioral Health Services

CBM: Curriculum Based Measures

CBT: Cognitive Behavioral Therapy

CC: Capitol Clubhouse

CCDF: Childcare and Development Fund

CCIDS: Center for Community Inclusion and Disability Studies

CCM: Community Case Manager

CCS: Clinical Care Specialist

CCS: Certified Clinical Supervisor

CCSME: Co-Occurring Collaborative Serving Maine

CCSP: Childcare Subsidy Program

CDC: Center for Disease Control & Prevention

CDC: Consent Decree Coordinator

CDS: Child Development Services

CEU: Continuing Education Unit

CFR: Code of Federal Regulations

CFS: Child and Family Services

CHAT: Children's Habilitation Assessment Tool

CHCS: Community Health and Counseling Services

CI: Community Integration

CHIP: Child Health Insurance Program

CIPSS: Certified Intentional Peer Support Specialist

CHADD: Children and Adults with Attention Deficit/Hyperactivity Disorder

CHAT: Children's Habilitation Assessment Tool.

CHC: Community Health Center

CHP: Comprehensive Health Planner

CMHC: Community Mental Health Center

CMMC: Central Maine Medical Center

CMO: Case Management Officer

CMS: Claims Management System

CMS: Center for Medicare and Medicaid Services

CNA: Certified Nurse's Assistant

COBRA: Consolidated Omnibus Budget Reconciliation Act of 1985
COLA: Cost of Living Adjustment
CPA: Child Placing Agency
CPS: Child Protective Services
COT: Council on Transition
CQI: Continuous Quality Improvement
CRMA: Certified Residential Medications Aide (cert to dispense meds)
CRT: Children's Review Team
CSD: Community School District
CSHN: Children with Special Health Needs
CSN: Community Service Network (DHHS healthcare districts)
CSP: Community Support Provider (a DHHS licensed agency)
CSS: Community Support Service (MaineCare rehabilitation service)
CSW: Community Support Worker (MaineCare language for case manager)
CW: Child Welfare
CW: Case Worker

D
DAB: Drug-Affected Baby
DAFS: Department of Administrative and Financial Services
DBA: Doing Business As
DBT: Dialectical Behavioral Therapy
DCF: Downeast Correctional Facility
DD: Development Delay
DDPC: Dorothea Dix Psychiatric Center
DDS: Disability Determination Services
DEA: Drug Enforcement Agency
DHHS: Department of Health & Human Services
DHS: Department of Human Services
DLS: Daily Living Skills
DME: Durable Medical Equipment
DMR: Division of Mental Retardation
DO: Doctor of Osteopathy

DOB: Date of Birth

DOC: Department of Corrections

DOD: Department of Defense and Veterans Affairs

DOE: Department of Education

DOL: Department of Labor

DON: Director of Nursing

DOT: Department of Transportation

DRC: Disability Rights Center

DROMBO: Division of Regional Office of Management and Budget Operations

DSA: Designated State Agency

DSM: Diagnostic & Statistical Manual

DSP: Direct Support Provider

DUR: Drug Utilization Review

DRM: Disability Rights Maine

DVM: Defense, Veterans, and Emergency Management

E

EA: Emergency Assistance

EAP: Employee Assistance Program

EBA: Evidenced-Based Practices

EBP: Evidence-Based Practice

EBT: Electronic Benefit Transfer

ECS: Early Childhood Services

ED: Emergency Department

ED: Executive Director

EFT: Electronic Funds Transfer

EHB: Essential Health Benefits

EHR: Electronic Health Record

EI: Early Intervention

EIM: Elder Independence of Maine

EIN: Employer Identification Number

EIS: Enterprise Information System

ELC: Elizabeth Levinson Center

ELL: English Language Learner

EMMC: Eastern Maine Medical Center
EMR: Electronic Medical Records
EMS: Emergency Medical Services
EMTLA: Emergency Medical Treatment and Active Labor Act
EOB: Explanation of Benefits
EOMB: Explanation of Medical Benefits or Explanation of Medicare Benefits
EPA: Environmental Protection Agency
EPSDT: Early Periodic Screening, Diagnosis & Testing
ERISA: Employee Retirement Income Security Act
ERS: Electronic Remittance Statement
ESL: English as a Second Language

F
FA: Functional Assessment
FAME: Financial Authority of Maine
FAMIS: Family Assistance Management Information System (now ACES)
FAPE: Free and Appropriate Public Education Act
FAS: Fetal Alcohol Syndrome
FBA: Functional Behavioral Assessment (same as FA)
FBI: Federal Bureau of Investigation
FDC: Family Drug Court
FEMA: Federal Emergency Management Agency
FERPA: Family Educational Rights and Privacy Act
FFS: Fee For Service
FFT: Functional Family Therapy
FFY: Federal Fiscal Year (Oct. 1 – Sept. 30)
FH: Foster Home
FHA: Federal Housing Administration
FIS: Family Information Specialist
FJA: Functional Job Analysis
FLRP: Federal Loan Repayment Program
FLSA: Fair Labor Standards Act

FMLA: Family Medical Leave Act
FMO: Fire Marshall's Office
FOIA: Freedom of Information Act
FTE: Full Time Equivalent
FP: Family Partners
FY: Fiscal Year (State of Maine: July 1- to June 30)

G
GA: General Assistance
GAAP: Generally Accepted Accounting Principles
GAL: Guardian ad Litem
GAO: General Accounting Office
GBSD: Governor Baxter School for the Deaf
GBSDMSDHH: Governor Baxter School for the Deaf Maine School for the Deaf and Hard of Hearing
G.E.A.R. Parent Network: Gaining Empowerment Allows Results (parent network)
GED: General Equivalency Degree
GO: Governor's Office
GO: Government Office
GHS: Goold Health Services
GSA: Government Services Administration
GSL: Guaranteed Student Loan Program

H
HBA: Health Benefits Advisor
HBC: Home Based Care
HCBS: Home and Community-Based Services
HCC: Health Care Center
HCF: Health Care Facility
HCCA: Home Care Coordinating Agency
HCT: Home & Community-Based Treatment (MaineCare service)
HEAP: Home Energy Assistance Program
HH: Health Homes (medical case management as part of ObamaCare/ACA)

HHA: Home Health Agency
HHA: Home Health Assistant
HHA: Home Health Aide
HHCS: Home Health Care Services
HHS: US Department of Health and Human Services
HHO: Health Home Organization
HIE: Health Information Exchange
HIN: Health Information Network
HIPAA: Health Insurance Portability & Accountability Act
HIPO: Health Insurance Premium Option
HIT: Health Information Technology
HIV: Human Immunodeficiency Virus
HMO: Health Maintenance Organization
HMS: Health Management Systems
HR: Human Resources
HRA: Health Reimbursement Account
HRSA: Health Resources and Services Administration
HAS: Health Savings Account
HUD: Housing and Urban Development

I
IADL: Instrumental Activities of Daily Living
IAP: Individual Accommodation Plan
IAU: Institutional Abuse Unit
ICD-9: International Classification of Diseases; used for mental health diagnosing
ICD-10: The most recent version of the ICD
ICF/MR: Intermediate Care Facility for Persons with Intellectual Disabilities.
ICF/MR-G: Intermediate Care Facility for Persons with Intellectual Disabilities with group needs
ICF/MR-N: Intermediate Care Facility for Persons with Intellectual Disabilities with nursing needs
ICM: Integrated Case Management

ICU: Intensive Care Unit
ID: Intellectual Disability (Mental Retardation)
IDEA: Individuals with Disabilities Education Act
IDEIA: Individuals with Disabilities Education Improvement Act
IDT: Interdisciplinary Team
IEP: Individual Education Plan
IEVS: Income and Eligibility Verification System
IF&W: Inland Fisheries and Wildlife
IFSP: Individual Family Service Plan
IJ: Immediate Jeopardy
IL: Independent Living
INS: Immigration and Naturalization Services
ISP: Individual Service/Support Plan
IST: Incompetent to Stand Trial
ITP: Individual Treatment Plan
ITRT: Intensive Temporary Residential Treatment

J
JAG: Judge Advocate General (military attorney/s)
JCAHO: Joint Commission on Accreditation of Healthcare Organizations
JCCO: Juvenile Community Correctional Officer
JJAG: Juvenile Justice Advisory Group
JOBS: Job Opportunities and Basic Skills

K
KBH: Kennebec Behavioral Health
KEPRO: Name of the third-party MaineCare utilization review system
KMCC: Keeping Maines Children Connected
KSA: Knowledge, Skills, and Abilities
KVCAP: Kennebec Valley Community Action Program

L
LADC: Licensed Alcohol Drug Counselor
LAN: Local Area Network

LCSW: Licensed Clinical Social Worker

LD: Learning Disability

LD: Legislative Document

LDA: Learning Disabilities Association

LEA: Local Education Agency

LEA: Local Law Enforcement Agency

LIHEAP: Low Income Home Energy Assistance Program

LFA: Lead Federal Agency

LMSW: Licensed Master of Social Work

LSW: Licensed Social Worker

LOC: Level of Care

LOCUM TENENS: A provider that substitutes for another provider

LOCUS: Level of Care Utilization System (Maine's version of ASAM)

LPC: Licensed Professional Counselor

LPN: Licensed Practical Nurse

LSAC: Licensed Substance Abuse Counselor

LSC: Life Safety Code

LSE: Legal Services for the Elderly

LSW: Licensed Social Worker

LTC: Long-Term Care

LTFC: Long Term Foster Care

M

MAAP: Maine Uniform Accounting and Auditing Practices

MACED: Maine Advisory Council on the Education of Children with Disabilities

MACSP: Maine Association of Community Service Providers

MACWIS: Maine Automated Child Welfare Information System

MADSEC: Maine Administrators of Services for Children with Disabilities

MAFAP: Maine Association of Foster and Adoptive Parents

MAFO: Maine Alliance of Family Organizations

MAMHS: Maine Association of Mental Health Services

MANP: Maine Association of Nonprofits

MAPSIS: Maine Adult Protective Services Information System

MASAP: Maine Association of Substance Abuse Providers

MATCH: Modular Approach to Therapy for Children (A.D.T.C: Anxiety, Depression, Trauma, & Conduct Problems)

MBHO: Maine Behavioral Health Organization

MBM: MaineCare Benefits Manual

MC: MaineCare

MCA: Maine Children's Alliance

MCBM: Maine Care Benefits Manual

MCD: Maine Center on Deafness

MCF: Maine Caring Families

MCLU: Maine Civil Liberties Union

MCO: Managed Care Organization

MD: Medical Doctor

MDA: Maine Dental Association

MDEA: Maine Drug Enforcement Agency

MDHA: Maine Dental Hygienists' Association

MDTFC: Multi-dimensional Treatment Foster Care

MEA: Maine Education Association

MeHAF: Maine Health Access Foundation

MEJ: Maine Equal Justice

MEJP: Maine Equal Justice Partners

MEMA: Maine Emergency Management Agency

MH: Mental Health

MHDO: Maine Health Data Organization

MHMR: Mental Health/Mental Retardation, renamed BDS, now combined with DHHS.

MHRA: Maine Human Rights Act

MHSS: Mental Health Support Specialist

MHRT1: Mental Health Rehabilitation Technician (mental health in home supports)

MHRTC: Mental Health Rehabilitation Technician for the Community

MI: Mental Illness

MI: Motivational Interviewing

MIHMS: Maine Integrated Health Management Solution

MHPC: Mental Health Program Coordinator
MMA: Maine Military Authority
MOU: Memorandum of Understanding
MPCA: Maine Primary Care Association
MPF: Maine Parent Federation
MR: Mental Retardation
MRSA: Maine Revised Statues Annotated
MSAD: Maine School Administrative District
MSEA: Maine State Employees Association
MSHA: Maine State Housing Authority
MSL: Maine State Library
MSLR: Maine State Learning Results
MSP: Maine State Police
MSP: Maine State Prison
MST: Multi-Systemic Therapy
MST-PSB: Multi-Systemic Therapy, Problem Sexual Behavior
MSW: Master of Social Work
MTN: Maine Transition Network

N
NAMI: National Alliance on Mental Illness
NAMI-MAINE: National Alliance on Mental Health of Maine
NCANDS: National Child Abuse/Neglect Data System
NCLB: Not Child Left Behind
NCR: Not Competent to Stand Trial
NEA: National Education Association
NF: Nursing Facility
NFI: NFI North, Incorporated
NH: Nursing Home
NIH: National Institute of Health
NIMH: National Institute of Mental Health
NP: Nurse Practitioner
NYTD: National Youth Transition Data Base

O

OADS: Office of Aging and Disability Services (adult protective services)

OBH: Office of Behavioral Health (formerly the Office of adult mental health and the Office of substance abuse)

OCD: Obsessive-Compulsive Disorder

OCFS: Office of Child & Family Services

OCR: Office of Civil Rights

ODD: Oppositional Defiant Disorder

OIG: Office of the Inspector General

OHH: Opioid Health Home (addiction version of BHH)

OJT: On-the-job- Training

OMB: Office of Management and Budget

OMS: Office of MaineCare Services

OP: Outpatient

OQMHP: Other Qualified Mental Health Professionals (children's case manager)

OSA: Office of Substance Abuse (now part of OBH)

OSHA: Occupational Safety and Health Administration

OT: Occupational Therapy

P

PA: Prior Authorization

PA: Physician's Assistant

PACE: Program of All-inclusive Care for the Elderly

PASARR: Pre-admission Screening Annual Resident Review

PCA: Personal Care Assistant

PCCM: Primary Care Case Management

PCHC: Penobscot Communty Health Center

PCMH: Patient-Centered Medical Home

PCP: Person Centered Plan

PCP: Primary Care Physician or Provider

PCS: Personal Care Services

PDD: Pervasive Developmental Disorder

PDD-NOS: Pervasive Developmental Disorder-Not Otherwise Specified

PDN: Private Duty Nurse

PHN: Public Health Nursing

PL: Public Law

PMP: Prescription Monitoring Program

PMPM: Per Member Per Month (the billing model for BHH)

PNMI: Private Non-Medical Institutions (MaineCare funded group home)

PO: Probation Officer

PO: Purchase Order

POC: Plan of Care

POC: Plan of Correction

PPE: Prospective Payment Exclusion

PPE: Personal Protective Equipment

PPO: Preferred Provider Organization

PT: Physical Therapy

PTL: Pine Tree Legal

PTSD: Post Traumatic Stress Disorder

Q

QA: Quality Assurance

QAPP: Quality Assurance Program Plan

QC: Quality Control

QI: Quality Improvement

QIA: Quality Improvement Activity

QIC: Quality Improvement Council

QMB: Qualified Medicare Beneficiaries

QRS: Quality Rating and Improvement System

QRIS: Quality Rating and Improvement System

R

RA: Remittance Advice

RCS: Rehabilitative and Community Services

RCF: Residential Care Facility
RFI: Request for Information
RFP: Request for Proposal
RGH: Rumford Group Homes
RN: Registered Nurse
RO: Regional Office
ROM: Results-Oriented Management System Out of the University of Kansas
RPC: Riverview Psychiatric Center
RSU: Regional School Unit
RTI: Response To Intervention

S
SA: Substance Abuse
SAD: School Administrative Unit
SAMHS: Office of Substance Abuse and Mental Health Services (now OBH)
SAMHSA: Substance Abuse and Mental Health Services Administration
SAU: School Administrative Unit
SB: School-Based
SBI: State Bureau of Investigation
SED: Severe Emotional Disturbance
SETU: State Education and Training Unit
SFMO: State Fire Marshall's Office
SFY: State Fiscal Year (July 1- June 30)
SIDS: Sudden Infant Death Syndrome
SLD: Specific Learning Disability
SLMB: Specified Low-income Medicare Beneficiaries
SMPA: Southern Maine Parent Awareness
SNF: Skilled Nursing Facility
SOC: System of Care
SOD: Statement of Deficiencies
SOP: Standard Operating Procedures
SOS: Secretary of State

SSA: Social Security Act
SSA: Social Security Administration
SSD: Social Security Disability
SSDI: Social Security Disability Income
SSI: Supplemental Security Income
SSN: Social Security Number
SSPI: Social Services Program Specialist I, II, III
SP: Speech Pathologist
ST: Speech Therapy
SUD: Substance Use Disorders
SURS: Surveillance, Utilization, and Review

T
T&A: Time and Attendance
TANF: Temporary Assistance for Needy Families
TBI: Traumatic Brain Injury
TCM: Targeted Case Management
TCMH: Tri-County Mental Health Services
TDD/TTY: Telecommunications Device for the Deaf
TFCBT: Trauma-Focused Cognitive Behavioral Therapy
TR: Therapeutic Recreation

U
UCMJ: Uniform Code of Military Justice (military law)
UCP: United Cerebral Palsy
UR: Utilization Review
USC: United States Code

V
VA: Veterans Affairs
VOA: Volunteers of America
VR: Division of Vocational Rehabilitation
VR: Vital Records
VS: Vital Statistics

W
WC: Worker's Compensation
WHO: World Health Organization
WIC: Woman, Infants & Children
WMD: Weapons of Mass Destruction
WWW: World Wide Web

Y
YDC: Youth Development Center
YMM: Youth MOVE Maine
Y-OQ: Youth Outcome Questionnaire
YTD: Year To Date

About the Author

Jason White is an assistant professor of social and behavioral sciences, within the University of Maine system. He is the former executive director of Maine Behavioral Health Organization; a statewide non-profit behavioral health organization that he developed and led for 10 years. Before that, Dr. White worked for the Maine Department of Health and Human Services, as a behavioral health agency licensing manager. He was also appointed by Maine's governor, to the Governor Baxter School for the Deaf and Maine Educational Center for the Deaf and Hard of Hearing school board and was later elected to the board chair position.

Professor White also served in the United States Army, and later as a commissioned officer in the Maine Army National Guard. Upon retiring in 2014, he published a book on his experiences in Iraq, as a platoon leader, in the State's revered engineer battalion. He is the recipient of multiple military awards, including good conduct, and the Combat Action Badge.

Dr. White's areas of expertise are behavioral health policy, and leader behavior, as evidenced by his experience and education. He has four degrees: AA in General Studies, BA in Social Science, MS in Educational Psychology (with a concentration in applied behavior analysis), and an EdD in Educational Leadership (with his dissertation focus on clinical leader behavior). Additionally, he holds numerous paraprofessional certifications and licenses and has his clinical licensure in substance use disorder treatment, and clinical supervision.

Back Cover

Developing regulatory-compliant mental health and substance use disorder assessments and treatment plans can be challenging, especially in the most difficult state to get licensed in, deliver services, and bill. In this book, the author walks the reader through the regulations, relevant policies, and common audit citations, to develop a regulatory-compliant mental health and substance use disorder client and patient treatment record.

www.ingramcontent.com/pod-product-compliance
Lightning Source LLC
Chambersburg PA
CBHW082359270326
41935CB00013B/1681